C000067451

Brighton & Hove Albion
ON THIS DAY

HISTORY, FACTS & FIGURES
FROM EVERY DAY OF THE YEAR

Brighton & Hove Albion
ON THIS DAY

HISTORY, FACTS & FIGURES
FROM EVERY DAY OF THE YEAR

DAN TESTER

Brighton & Hove Albion
ON THIS DAY
HISTORY, FACTS & FIGURES
FROM EVERY DAY OF THE YEAR

All statistics, facts and figures are correct as of 30th September 2007

© Dan Tester

John Northcutt has asserted his rights in accordance with the Copyright, Designs and
Patents Act 1988 to be identified as the author of this work.

Published By:

Pitch Publishing (Brighton) Ltd

A2 Yeoman Gate

Yeoman Way

Durrington

BN13 3QZ

Email: info@pitchpublishing.co.uk

Web: www.pitchpublishing.co.uk

First published 2007

A catalogue record for this book is available from the British Library.

10-digit ISBN: 1-9054111-0-3

13-digit ISBN: 978-1-9054111-0-8

Printed and bound in Great Britain by Cromwell Press

THIS BOOK IS DEDICATED TO MY GRANDFATHER, RON,
AND MY FATHER, PAUL, FOR INTRODUCING ME
TO ANOTHER AMAZING FAMILY.

Dan Tester – September 2007

FOREWORD BY PAUL ROGERS

When I first came to play for the Albion, I was aware of the club's impressive history. When I was growing up as a young football fan the team were in the first division and it's because of this I have always considered Brighton to be a big team – so it was fantastic to get the chance to come and play for the club and subsequently help them back up to a higher level.

Several of the games across those two memorable championship-winning seasons are featured in these pages – including, of course, the Chesterfield game in 2001, which thanks to Danny Cullip's header was an unforgettable night under the lights at Withdean. I'm sure if Danny hadn't struck we still would have won the league with ease, but it was nice to clinch it on the night we played our main rivals.

Then there's the second championship win, clinched with a draw at home with Swindon. Some 36 years had passed without an Albion skipper lifting a trophy – and then suddenly I was lucky enough to lift two in the space of 12 months! That was thanks to a fantastic squad over the two years and two very good managers in Micky Adams and Peter Taylor.

Good players and managers are a feature of the book, with plenty of other stand-out dates featuring matches and events from the club's history. Despite having retired from professional football, I'm still lucky enough to be involved with the club as we move to Falmer – and hopefully Dan Tester will soon be writing a few more words on memorable days at our new stadium.

Paul Rogers, Brighton & Hove Albion 1999-2003

INTRODUCTION

Brighton & Hove Albion: On This Day chronicles the fascinating facts, figures, and trivia, for each date of the year concerning the club many of us love: Brighton & Hove Albion FC.

The Albion has enjoyed many amazing highs, and a fair few lows, in its colourful 106-year history. The book starts on January 1st and follows the action on every date through to December 31st. FA Cup giant-killings are prominent at the beginning and as we enter April the excitement of promotion run-ins, championships – and relegation battles – intensifies. May sees magical FA Cup final appearances, the do-or-die drama of Hereford and play-off success. Summer month activity is more subdued, with new faces arriving and old ones departing for pastures new. August explodes into life as new seasons kick off rife with unbridled optimism for what lies ahead…and, after a few months, perhaps pessimism! Incredible matches, amazing scorelines, fantastic individual feats, unusual goings-on, remarkable players, successive .championships, first division highlights, Cup runs – and unscrupulous businessmen – are all featured throughout.

Many an hour has been spent trawling through newspaper archives at the Brighton History Library, decades worth of old programmes, and the excellent books by Paul Camillin, Tim Carder and Roger Harris, to bring you this book. It's been a fantastic and educational experience putting it together, and I sincerely hope you enjoy reading *Albion: On This Day* as much I enjoyed writing it.

Dan Tester – September 2007

ACKNOWLEDGEMENTS

I'd like to express my gratitude to all those at Pitch Publishing, most notably Richard Walker, for the excellent editing job, and Roy Chuter for his expert knowledge of the Albion and proof reading. Huge thanks also to another Albion expert: Tim Carder – not only for his invaluable works: *Albion A-Z: A Who's Who of Brighton & Hove Albion FC* and *Seagulls! The Story of Brighton & Hove Albion FC*, both co-written with the late Roger Harris – but also for answering my many emails and phone calls. Thanks to Paul Rogers for leading Albion to two championships and also for writing the foreword; Tim, Rob, Roger and Bonnie for being fantastic office mates; Peter Foulkes, for the loan of his books and terrific encouragement; everyone who has contributed to the Albion matchday programme over the last forty years or so; the Battle of Trafalgar crew, especially Chris Jones; Albion press officer Paul Camillin for *The Brighton & Hove Albion Miscellany* and for his help and advice; and last, but by no means least: thanks to Klara, for her love, support and, above all, her patience.

Dan Tester – September 2007

Brighton & Hove Albion
ON THIS DAY

JANUARY

SATURDAY 1st JANUARY 1966

Eastville outfit Bristol Rovers were the New Year's Day opponents at the Goldstone Ground. A brace from West Ham-born Charlie Livesey – and one each from Brain Tawse and Wally Gould – earned the Albion two points in front of 14,408 fans.

SATURDAY 1st JANUARY 1994

After signing on Christmas Day 1993, a crowd of 9,753 was at the Goldstone Ground to witness 39-year-old Jimmy Case's second debut for Albion. Kurt Nogan stole the show with a hat-trick in the impressive 4-1 thumping of Cambridge United with Brighton-born Simon Funnell netting the other goal. Future Seagull Steve Claridge was on target for the visitors.

SATURDAY 2nd JANUARY 1909

'Mr Albion' Charlie Webb made his Albion debut, and scored in the 1-1 draw at West Ham United. Born in Ireland in 1886, the inside-left scored 79 goals in 275 Albion appearances. Amazingly, Charlie managed the club for nearly 30 years after World War I – a total of 1,215 matches – and eventually retired, aged 60, in 1948 after a year as general manager. Charlie, much-loved and respected throughout the game, passed away in 1973. A tree planted in his honour in Hove Park is still going strong.

SUNDAY 2nd JANUARY 1966

Kevan Brown was born in Hampshire. The right-back played 65 matches for Albion in the late 80s. He won the FA Trophy three times with Woking where he once inadvertently caused a match abandonment by falling into a two-foot deep hole that suddenly appeared in the pitch!

SATURDAY 2nd JANUARY 1993

After disposing of Hayes and Woking in the previous two rounds, Albion entertained south coast rivals Portsmouth in the FA Cup third round. Lethal strike duo Paul Walsh and Guy Whittingham were sidelined for the visitors through injury. Matthew Edwards scored the only goal of the tie to earn a trip to Manchester United in the next round.

MONDAY 3rd JANUARY 1916

A decade into his 16-year distinguished Albion career, Bert Longstaff received a letter from West Ham United inviting him to 'come and play for us whenever you possibly can on Saturdays'. The Irons helpfully pointed out that their players are insured for £2 per week.

SATURDAY 3rd JANUARY 1981

Albion's visit to Old Trafford attracted 42,199 for this FA Cup third round tie. Brian Horton and Red Devils old boy Andy Ritchie both hit the net. Future Seagull Mickey Thomas and England international Mike Duxbury score for Manchester United.

SATURDAY 3rd JANUARY 2000

Brighton-born striker Darren Freeman scored the first goal of the new Millennium in English professional football. The 26-year-old netted after just two minutes in the 4-2 third division home victory over Exeter City.

SATURDAY 3rd JANUARY 2005

Watford visited Withdean Stadium. Cuckfield-born Kerry Mayo flicked Albion level before Leon Knight completed the scoring for a 2-1 victory.

SATURDAY 4th JANUARY 1975

After despatching Aldershot and Brentford at the Goldstone Ground in the opening two rounds, Albion were at home again in the third round, this time against non-league Leatherhead. Peter Taylor's men were beaten by a Chris Kelly – the 'Leatherhead Lip' – strike. The only goal of the contest secured a fourth round trip to Leicester City's Filbert Street.

SATURDAY 4th JANUARY 1992

second division Albion hosted Southern Premier Division Crawley Town in an all-Sussex FA Cup third round encounter at the Goldstone Ground. Goals from Mark 'Smokey' Gall, Clive 'Flash' Walker, 'Free' Raphael Meade and an Ian 'Chappers' Chapman brace set up a fourth round clash with Bolton Wanderers at Burnden Park.

Saturday 5th January 1901

Brighton & Hove Rangers hosted Willesden Town at Withdean. A Gibson, a man of 'exciting credentials', played his part in a 6-2 thrashing of the north Londoners.

Saturday 5th January 1952

Just under 20,000 cold Albion fans are present at the Goldstone Ground for the Division Three (South) visit of Southend United. The second Billy Reed to represent the club – the first played 21 times in the 1914/15 campaign – netted twice; and Scot Johnny McNichol, left-back Jack Mansell and groundsman-to-be Frankie Howard all grabbed one each to give their team a resounding 5-0 victory.

Wednesday 5th January 1972

Colwyn Bay-born Peter O'Sullivan made his second appearance for the Welsh Under-23's in the 2-0 defeat against England at Swindon Town's County Ground.

Tuesday 5th January 1982

Failure to conquer the famous sloping pitch or the mud at Barnet's Underhill meant a FA Cup third round replay at the Goldstone. It was much less of an uphill struggle this time around as Albion canter through 3-1 thanks to a Neil McNab penalty and efforts from Mickey Thomas and Jimmy Case.

Monday 5th January 1987

Barry Lloyd is appointed Albion manager. The Middlesex-born former midfielder was on the bench for Fulham in the 1975 FA Cup Final and ended his playing career at Yeovil Town in 1979. Alan Mullery, a former team-mate at Craven Cottage, recruited his friend as reserve and youth team coach before the ex-England captain's sacking eight months later. It took 15 games for the 38-year-old to record his first victory; a 2-0 home win over Crystal Palace on Easter Monday.

Saturday 5th January 1991

The Albion announced that each fan pays 53 pence towards policing at the Goldstone Ground, putting the club in the top six in the country.

SATURDAY 6th JANUARY 1883

Legendary goalkeeper Bob Whiting was born in West Ham, east London. The six-foot-tall custodian impressed the Goldstone faithful with his kicking ability and is once said to have cleared the opposition crossbar from his own area! He made 320 appearances.

SATURDAY 6th JANUARY 1900

Albion predecessors Brighton United entertained Bedminster at the County Ground in Hove. The Greenbacks managed just one goal to the visitors' four. *The Argus* takes up the action... 'From the re-start Baker got away and forced a corner. Taking the kick himself, he placed the leather finely, and (Jock) Malloch, jumping up, headed the ball into the net amid a terrific shout of applause'.

MONDAY 6th JANUARY 1908

Albion travelled to Leyton, not to be confused with the modern day Orient, for a Western League Division One fixture. Stocky Scottish forward Donald Ronaldson scored Albion's goal in a 6-1 thrashing.

SATURDAY 6th JANUARY 1951

With Tooting & Mitcham and Ipswich Town swept aside, Albion entertained Chesterfield at home in the FA Cup third round. The powerful and prolific forward Ken Bennett – 41 goals in 107 appearances – scored, as did Johnny McNichol.

SATURDAY 6th JANUARY 1990

Without a home victory in any competition since a 1-0 second division win over Watford three months earlier, Albion fans were hoping for a turnaround in fortunes with the visit of first division Luton Town for a FA Cup third round encounter. They weren't disappointed! Defender Keith Dublin, midfielders Alan Curbishley and Robert Codner, and striker Garry Nelson plundered the goals to seal a 4-1 Goldstone victory.

SATURDAY 6th JANUARY 2007

Albion travelled to Premiership West Ham United for a FA Cup third round tie. Argentinean Carlos Tevez is man-of-the-match in a convincing 3-0 victory for the Hammers.

SATURDAY 7th JANUARY 1922

It was FA Cup day on the south coast as Albion hosted first division Sheffield United in this first round fixture. Wally Little, three years into a decade of service with the club, scored the only goal in front of 15,238 Goldstone fans.

SATURDAY 7th JANUARY 1911

Albion moved up to third in the Southern League Division One table with a 5-0 thrashing of Watford. Charlie Webb and Jimmy Smith both struck twice – and William 'Bullet' Jones once – to give a resounding victory to John Robson's men.

SATURDAY 7th JANUARY 1961

second division Albion and Derby County met at the Goldstone for a FA Cup third round tie. Forwards Ian McNeill, Bobby Laverick and Dennis Windross got the goals in a 3-1 win.

SATURDAY 7th JANUARY 1967

Albion thumped Southern League Bath City 5-0 in a Goldstone second round FA Cup match. Local boy Eric Whittington grabbed two, as does Scot Brian Tawse, and Dave Turner netted once.

WEDNESDAY 7th JANUARY 1981

David Coleman commentated on the Albion from the Goldstone for the first time for the BBC's Sportsnight show. Manchester United won the FA Cup third round reply 2-0 in front of 26,915. It was the second of three games against the Red Devils in seven days.

THURSDAY 7th JANUARY 1982

'Super' Bas Savage was born in London. The tall striker's career had been quite ordinary before his move to Withdean with just two goals in 64 appearances with Reading, Wycombe Wanderers, Bury, Bristol City and Gillingham. That was soon to change…six goals in 15 run-outs towards the end of 2006/07 was a healthy return. Bas endeared himself not just to Albion fans, but football supporters across the land, with his unique 'moonwalk' goal celebration. It became so popular it was regularly featured on Soccer AM, won a magazine award and spawned a successful range of T-shirts.

SATURDAY 8th JANUARY 1921

For the first time as a Football League club, Albion entered the FA Cup. Nearly 17,000 fans were at the Goldstone for the visit of first division Oldham Athletic and went home happy as Zacky March (2), Jack Doran and George Coomber struck in a 4-1 victory.

SATURDAY 8th JANUARY 1983

Albion drew 1-1 at home to second division Newcastle United in the FA Cup third round. Terry McDermott equalised for the Magpies after Andy Ritchie had put Albion ahead in the second half.

SATURDAY 8th JANUARY 2005

Over 5,000 Albion fans crammed into White Hart Lane for a third round FA Cup tie. Richard Carpenter levelled the scores with an excellent second-half free-kick but Robbie Keane's classy late winner sent Spurs into the next round.

SATURDAY 9th JANUARY 1943

Having scored seven goals in 20 Liverpool games at the onset of World War II, Northumbrian John Shafto guested for the Albion during the hostilities and banged in four against Luton Town.

SATURDAY 9th JANUARY 1946

Four days after a 2-1 win at Carrow Road in a FA Cup third round, first leg fixture, Albion hosted their first second leg match in the competition. Charlie Chase, Jock Davie (2) and Bert Stephens smashed in four to Norwich's one to set up a tie with Aldershot.

SATURDAY 9th JANUARY 1965

Flintshire-born Barrie Rees made his Albion debut in the 3-1 fourth division home win over Crewe Alexandra. Tragically, the young winger would only make a further 11 appearances in the club's colours before being killed in a car accident.

TUESDAY 9th JANUARY 2001

Utility man Adam Virgo made his debut in the Associate Members Cup 2-2 draw at Brentford. Albion lost on penalties in a game which was switched to Griffin Park from Withdean.

SATURDAY 10th JANUARY 1942

A crowd of 2,500 were at the Goldstone for a War South contest with Fulham. They went home disappointed as Albion were humbled 7-3!

TUESDAY 10th JANUARY 1942

Northern Ireland midfielder Danny Wilson signed permanently from Nottingham Forest after a six-week loan spell, in a £45,000 deal.

TUESDAY 10th JANUARY 1948

Fratton Park was the venue for this south coast derby in the FA Cup third round. Pompey were flying in the first division while Albion languished at the bottom of third division (south). The travelling supporters were not expecting to witness progression in the competition and were right. The Sussex boys lost 4-1 to their Hampshire counterparts who would go on to win the first division title in the next two seasons.

SATURDAY 10th JANUARY 1987

Dean Saunders replacement Richard Tiltman made his Albion debut in the 0-0 FA Cup third round draw at Sheffield United.

TUESDAY 11th JANUARY 1938

Freddie Jones was born in Caerphilly, Wales. The outside-left was signed from Arsenal for £5,000 in 1958 and was a regular in Albion's second division side for two seasons, making 76 starts and scoring 15 times.

SATURDAY 11th JANUARY 1964

Edgeley Park, Stockport, was the location for Wally Gould's debut in an Albion shirt. The Yorkshireman was a popular figure, marauding down the Goldstone flanks, and netted an impressive 46 times in 193 run-outs. He was released in February 1968 to embark on a successful career in South African football.

SATURDAY 11th JANUARY 1992

Barnsley were the visitors to Hove. Both teams, in the play-off chase the previous season, were in danger of heading out the division in the wrong direction. John Robinson, Brian Wade and Ian Chapman fired the Albion out of the relegation zone in front of 6,107 fans.

TUESDAY 12th JANUARY 1926

Albion held a 'Coming of Age' dinner (albeit a few months late) to celebrate 21 years of the limited company that is Brighton & Hove Albion, which was established in 1904.

SATURDAY 12th JANUARY 1935

Arsenal – who went on to win their third successive championship later in the season – were the visitors for a FA Cup third round tie. The north London club were such a massive draw that spectators were genuinely put off by fears of a crush in the ground and in the event the attendance was only 22,343 – 10,000 fewer than the record gate set two years earlier against West Ham United. The Gunners won 2-0.

SATURDAY 12th JANUARY 1963

The biggest freeze of the 20th century was playing havoc with the fixture list. Director Harold Paris borrowed a tarmacadam melting machine from Brighton Corporation to help thaw the Goldstone pitch. Crystal Palace were the visitors for what was one of only four games in the country to survive. The pitch was a quagmire and a goal from Peter Donnelly was not enough to prevent a 2-1 defeat.

SUNDAY 12th JANUARY 1975

Junior McDougald was born in Big Spring, Texas, to a US airman and an English mother. Released by Tottenham Hotspur, the forward joined Albion in 1994 and top-scored in his two seasons on the south coast before moving to Rotherham United.

WEDNESDAY 12th JANUARY 1983

After a 1-1 draw at the Goldstone the previous Saturday, Albion made the long journey north for this FA Cup third round replay at Newcastle. Over 32,000 Geordies did their best to unsettle Albion but it didn't stop Peter Ward firing home a left-footed effort on 62 minutes – his 95th and final goal for the club. The home side had two 'goals' disallowed in the last four minutes and Albion were through…

THURSDAY 12th JANUARY 1984

A group of players and directors paid for presents and visited Chailey Heritage to host a party for 120 youngsters.

WEDNESDAY 13th JANUARY 1971

Flying winger Peter O'Sullivan made his Wales Under-23 debut as substitute in a 1-0 defeat in Swansea.

SATURDAY 13th JANUARY 1973

Chelsea were the visitors for a third round FA Cup tie. The occasion was marred as violence broke out on the terraces. On the pitch, Albion lost 2-0; left-back George Ley and Chelsea's Ron 'Chopper' Harris were sent off in front of the 29,287 crowd.

SATURDAY 14th JANUARY 1911

In Yorkshire, Leeds City were dispatched 3-1 in a FA Cup first round tie. Bullet Jones (2) and Jimmy Smith – who scored 40 times in just 65 appearances – were the scorers. On arrival at Brighton station in the early hours of Sunday morning, 2,000 ecstatic locals belted out 'Good Old Brighton by the Sea' to their returning heroes.

SATURDAY 14th JANUARY 1961

Albion beat Liverpool 3-1 in a second division contest at the Goldstone. Recent signing from Chelsea, striker Tony Nicholas, centre-forward Dennis Windross and defender Roy Jennings scored the goals.

SATURDAY 15th JANUARY 1995

Albion's team that draw 3-3 with AFC Bournemouth at the Goldstone Ground did not cost a single penny. Nicky Rust, Danny Simmonds, Ian Chapman, Colin Pates, Steve Foster, Paul McCarthy, Mark Flatts, Jimmy Case, Kurt Nogan, Simon Funnell and Matthew Edwards all graduated from the youth system, were loan signings or free transfers.

SATURDAY 16th JANUARY 1982

Skipper Steve Foster played for 85 minutes with a broken nose after a collision with David Cross in the 1-0 home win over West Ham.

WEDNESDAY 16th JANUARY 1991

Newcastle United were the visitors to the Goldstone Ground on a wet and miserable evening. The 7,684 fans in attendance were treated to a four-goal salvo from home debutant Bryan Wade, who netted all the goals in the 4-2 victory. Wade scored nine times in 22 Albion games.

SATURDAY 17th JANUARY 1971

Pat Saward's 'Buy-a-Player Fund' (which resulted in the purchase of Bert Murray) was boosted by a match between an Albion side – which included Jimmy Tarbuck – and Eastbourne United. The comedian missed a penalty in a 3-2 United victory.

SATURDAY 17th JANUARY 1976

Colchester United were thumped 6-0 at the Goldstone. Ian Mellor, Andy Rollings, Fred Binney (2) and Gerry Fell (2) were the scorers as Peter Taylor's men moved back into second place in the third division.

SATURDAY 17th JANUARY 1981

Goalkeeper Perry Digweed made the first of his 201 appearances for Albion. The Chelsea-born custodian was signed from Fulham for £150,000 in 1981 by Alan Mullery and was 'Player of the Year' in the 1990/91 campaign which ended in the play-off final at Wembley.

MONDAY 18th JANUARY 1993

Just 1,664 fans turned up for the Autoglass Trophy match against Walsall at the Goldstone. Gary Chivers and Andy Kennedy scored in extra time to earn a 4-2 victory.

SATURDAY 18th JANUARY 1958

Hove-born Adrian Thorne scored on his Albion debut against Southend United at the Goldstone. He attended Brighton, Hove and Sussex Grammar School and signed on his 17th birthday in August 1954.

SUNDAY 19th JANUARY 1890

George Coomber was born in West Hoathly, Sussex. On moving to London to complete a glass-blowing apprenticeship, the half-back turned out for Tufnell Park. George played for Watford and Spurs during the Great War and eventually started for the Albion in 1919, going on to score six times in 272 appearances.

SATURDAY 19th JANUARY 1980

Nearly 30,000 fans were at the Goldstone for the first division visit of Tottenham Hotspur. After consecutive 2-0 away wins – at Mansfield Town and Bolton Wanderers – Albion went down by the same score.

Monday 20th January 1908

The Albion travelled to Stamford Bridge for a Monday afternoon game at two-times league champions Preston North End in a FA Cup first round Second Replay. The 20,000 crowd was the largest, at this time, to watch the club. Dick Wombwell netted the decisive goal and the team were mobbed by ecstatic fans on their return to Brighton Station.

Tuesday 20th January 1925

Geoff Pinchbeck was born in Cleethorpes. The centre-forward joined from first division Everton for £2,000 in 1949. Five goals – and 14 starts – later, Port Vale splashed out £3,500. A tidy profit in three months!

Sunday 20th January 1974

Albion played Sunday football for the first time at the Goldstone as part of an experiment during a period of national crisis: a state of emergency had been declared as industrial unrest brought the country to its knees. The biggest crowd of the season – 18,885 – saw goals from Tony Towner and Ken Beamish secure a 2-1 win over Rochdale. The fans didn't pay for entry – it was illegal to charge. Instead, they paid a subscription to become members of the 'Dolphins Club' for the day. A turnstile was provided for those reluctant to pay anything.

Wednesday 21st January 1987

Twenty or so hardy fans helped clear the pitch and terraces of snow before the FA Cup third round replay with Sheffield United. The 7,019 crowd saw Dale Jasper score for Albion in the 2-1 defeat.

Saturday 21st January 2006

Albion lost 3-1 at Bramall Lane in the Championship. The result was one of only three defeats in 13 competitive fixtures played on this day in the club's history. Ten victories include a 5-0 mauling of Gillingham in 1956. Albion have won seven of their nine away games on January 21st.

Friday 22nd January 1999

Manager Brian Horton left Albion for a second time, to join first division side Port Vale. In 43 games under the former club captain the record reads: won 14, drawn 10 and lost 19. Horton's assistant Jeff Wood was put in temporary charge.

SATURDAY 23rd JANUARY 1965

Robert Codner was born in Walthamstow, London. With 47 goals in 315 run-outs, predominantly in the second tier, the midfielder was one of the most frustrating players in the club's history. Codner divided opinion among the fans soon after manager Barry Lloyd outbid Millwall for the Barnet player's services in 1988.

SATURDAY 23rd JANUARY 1982

Keith Cassells tore lacklustre Albion apart as third division Oxford United stuffed their first division counterparts 3-0 at the Goldstone in the FA Cup fourth round. The result provoked this response from an unhappy punter in *The Evening Argus* classified ads section: '11 clockwork clowns for sale'. The club's telephone number was quoted!

SATURDAY 23rd JANUARY 1993

Ryan Giggs scored the only goal of the game as Manchester United beat Albion in the FA Cup fourth round in front of 33,610 Old Trafford spectators.

SATURDAY 24th JANUARY 1931

For the fifth time in seven years, Albion played Watford in the FA Cup. They were beaten 2-0 in front of 22,700 supporters at Vicarage Road.

THURSDAY 24th JANUARY 2002

Albion wilted in front of the Sky TV cameras at Griffin Park. Steve Sidwell and Ivar Ingimarsson scored for Brentford in the 4-0 rout.

SATURDAY 25th JANUARY 1930

Confidence buoyed by consecutive 1-0 away victories, 8,000 Albion fans travelled west to Fratton Park. First division Pompey were no match for the rampaging Hugh Vallance whose goal decided the FA Cup fourth round tie.

SATURDAY 25th JANUARY 1969

Eddie Spearritt made his Albion debut in the 1-1 Goldstone third division draw with Crewe Alexandra. The 21-year-old utility player signed from Ipswich Town for £20,000 and went on to score 25 times in 232 appearances.

SATURDAY 26th JANUARY 1963

This was only Albion's second fixture this month due to the atrocious freezing weather. Most of the 11,633 Goldstone crowd wished they'd stayed at home as it's a goalless draw with Southend United.

SATURDAY 26th JANUARY 1980

Albion lost 2-0 at Arsenal in the FA Cup fourth round. It was the fifth meeting between the two sides that season; two league defeats, one League Cup loss and a 0-0 draw. Albion failed to score while the Gunners netted 13 times!

SATURDAY 26th JANUARY 1991

Nearly 7,000 Sussex folk wiped their eyes in disbelief as Albion came back from 2-0 down at Anfield. A penalty by Mike Small, after defender Paul McCarthy was fouled, and a late John Byrne header earned a FA Cup replay with champions Liverpool at the Goldstone. The game will be forever remembered for John 'Football Genius' Crumplin's superb marshalling of England international winger John Barnes.

SATURDAY 27th JANUARY 1906

Around 4,000 fans were at the Goldstone Ground for the Southern League Division One visit of Brentford. Billy Yates – in his only season on the coast – found the net along with Harry Kent and Proctor Hall.

SATURDAY 27th JANUARY 1951

Ashton Gate, home of Bristol City, was the setting for this 1-0 fourth round FA Cup exit.

SATURDAY 27th JANUARY 1990

Albion bowed out of the FA Cup with a 2-1 reverse on the plastic pitch at Oldham Athletic's Boundary Park.

SATURDAY 27th JANUARY 2007

An unremarkable League One scoreless draw continued an unwanted statistic: Albion have never won on January 27th in their 87-year league history. No more than one goal has been scored in five draws and seven defeats.

WEDNESDAY 28th JANUARY 1920

Frank Morrad was born in Middlesex. The non-attacking full-back worked as a part-time bookmaker and joined Albion after failing to hold down a first-team berth at Fulham. He made his debut against Aldershot in February 1948 and would appear intermittently over the next four seasons.

SATURDAY 28th JANUARY 1922

Huddersfield Town – who would bag a hat-trick of successive league titles under the expert tutelage of Herbert Chapman in the mid-20s – attractted the highest Goldstone gate so far of 22,241. The FA Cup second round tie ended goalless. The season's average was 8,095.

SATURDAY 28th JANUARY 1928

A gate of just 4,494 was registered at the Goldstone for the visit of Crystal Palace. The rivalry was not as keen in the 20s and Albion's average crowd was around the 7,500 mark. Despite the low attendance, the Hove side ran out 4-2 winners in the third division (south) fixture with Tug Wilson grabbing a brace.

SATURDAY 28th JANUARY 1961

One of the most celebrated games in Albion history. Visitors Burnley were reigning Football League champions and their fourth round FA Cup trip to Hove attracted a 28,672 gate. The 3-3 draw included goals from Jack Bertolini, Bob McNicol and Dennis Windross. Right-back McNicol's strike was one of the greatest ever seen at the Goldstone; a 35-yard rocket after a run from his own half. It was his only goal for the club!

SATURDAY 28th JANUARY 1967

Two special trains ferried Albion fans to the Recreation Ground, Aldershot, for a FA Cup third round tie. The fourth division Hampshire side held their third division opponents to a 0-0 draw in front of 12,812 spectators.

SATURDAY 28th JANUARY 1978

Albion's FA Cup fourth round tie with Notts County was postponed due to a waterlogged pitch. Seven hundred fans from Nottinghamshire are stranded in Hove after their special train could not be stopped in time.

SATURDAY 29th JANUARY 1927

After scoring 41 goals in the previous 13 Goldstone encounters, the omens were good for the 7,472 fans in attendance for the visit of Bristol Rovers. A 2-0 half-time lead gave no indication of the second-half avalanche that was to follow as inside-left Jimmy Hopkins, with a hat-trick, Tommy Cook and centre-half Paul Mooney added to inside-right Sam Jennings' first-half brace to make it 7-0!

SATURDAY 29th JANUARY 1955

After signing from Sussex County League Shoreham, Johnny Trusler made his only Albion appearance in the 3-1 defeat at Exeter City.

SATURDAY 29th JANUARY 1966

In the last seven Goldstone fixtures 27 Albion goals had been scored and the third division visit of Mansfield Town continued the trend. Brian Tawse (2), centre-forward Jack Smith – 36 strikes in 96 run-outs – and Charlie Livesey fired the Albion into a 5-2 interval lead. Despite a spirited fight-back the Stags went down 6-4.

SATURDAY 29th JANUARY 1983

The last time Manchester City had visited the Goldstone they had lost 4-1. Going into the FA Cup fourth round game Albion had recorded the only victory in their previous nine games: the FA Cup replay win at Newcastle. One place off the bottom of the first division Brighton fans were due a lift and it duly arrived when Jimmy Case opened the scoring before Michael Robinson netted twice against his former club. Neil Smillie added one more to better last year's scoreline: 4-0 to the Albion. Elsewhere the programme highlighted Mike Bamber's meeting with Brighton Borough Council regarding proposals for a new stadium.

SUNDAY 29th JANUARY 1984

The live TV cameras – a rarity in these days – were present for the visit of champions Liverpool for this FA Cup fourth round tie at the Goldstone Ground. Tony Grealish found Gerry Ryan with a lofted pass in the 57th minute and the Irishman dinked the ball home. Just a minute later and a slide-rule pass found Terry Connor galloping through to finish from just outside the box. Another memorable Albion victory over Liverpool.

SATURDAY 30th JANUARY 1937

Albion beat Bristol Rovers in a third division (south) fixture. Alec Law – who scored 40 goals in 74 appearances – scored, along with Joe Wilson, Hugh Stephens and Bobby Farrell (2) to make it 5-2.

WEDNESDAY 30th JANUARY 1991

After coming back from 2-0 down at champions Liverpool to gallantly draw 2-2 in the FA Cup fourth round, Albion entertained the best team in the land at the Goldstone Ground. England international midfielder Steve McMahon fired the Reds ahead before Mike Small ran through the static defence to slot home a first-half equaliser. Extra-time ensued and it was John Byrne who raced on to a misplaced pass to fire across Bruce Grobbelaar to send the North Stand into raptures. Unfortunately, a famous win was not forthcoming as Ian Rush – with a great finish into the top corner – and McMahon again, with a tap in, gave the Merseysiders a 3-2 victory.

WEDNESDAY 31st JANUARY 1906

F Harding, W G Edwards and Dick Kitto made their one and only appearances for the Albion in a 0-0 United League home draw with Clapton Orient.

WEDNESDAY 31st JANUARY 1934

After defeating Swindon Town 3-1 at the Goldstone in the third round, Albion headed north to Bolton Wanderers – three-times winners in the previous decade – for a FA Cup replay after a 1-1 draw. Things don't go according to plan as the Trotters hit the Albion for six. Brighton's goal in the 6-1 drubbing was even scored by a Bolton player!

SATURDAY 31st JANUARY 1942

Jock Davey bagged five goals in the 8-2 London War League victory against Chelsea at the Goldstone Ground.

SATURDAY 31st JANUARY 1953

Roy Jennings, club captain from 1960 to 1964, made the first of his 297 Albion appearances. The Swindon-born defender, who spent six years at full-back before converting to a more central berth, netted 22 times in his 12 years on the coast.

Brighton & Hove Albion

ON THIS DAY

FEBRUARY

WEDNESDAY 1st FEBRUARY 1908

Southern League Albion enjoyed a two-day stay in Birkdale before playing Liverpool at Anfield in the FA Cup. A penalty from Jack Hall was cancelled out by the Reds' late equaliser. The players alighted their train at Preston Park to avoid a huge crowd of fans at Brighton Station!

SATURDAY 1st FEBRUARY 1913

Around 11,000 rain-soaked Goldstone fans watched a second round FA Cup tie – which Everton offered to switch to Goodison Park for bigger gate receipts – that ended goalless.

WEDNESDAY 1st FEBRUARY 1967

Goals from Eric Whitington, Kit Napier and Charlie Livesey – the first by an Albion sub – sealed a 3-1 FA Cup victory over Aldershot. The prospect of a fourth round tie against first division Chelsea attracted a Goldstone crowd of 29,208, generating record gate receipts of £6,250.

SATURDAY 1st FEBRUARY 2003

Big Dave Beasant made his Albion debut in the 1-0 Championship defeat at Walsall. The Wimbledon FA Cup winner celebrated his 44th birthday while at the club and made 16 appearances.

SATURDAY 2nd FEBRUARY 1924

One of Albion's most famous victories… Everton were the visitors to Hove for a second round FA Cup fixture. The record crowd of 27,450 saw Albion tear apart a team that included six internationals. A hat-trick from Tommy Cook, a penalty from Wally Little and a late goal from Andy Neil sealed an astonishing 5-2 win.

MONDAY 2nd FEBRUARY 1982

Littlehampton Town won the Sussex County five-a-side tournament at the Brighton Centre. Albion beat Southampton 3-0 in the exhibition match with goals from Neil McNab and two from Gary Stevens.

THURSDAY 2nd FEBRUARY 1922

Jimmy Sirrell was born in Glasgow. The inside-forward scored 17 times in 58 Albion starts and would go on to take Notts County from fourth division to the First in three spells as boss.

SATURDAY 3rd FEBRUARY 1906

Big-spending Middlesbrough – who had purchased Alf Common in the first ever £1,000 signing the previous year – offered to stage this second round FA Cup tie at Ayresome Park. Albion's management declined. Goldstone admission was doubled to 1 shilling (5p) and 7,462 came through the turnstiles. The match finished 1-1 with Jimmy Kennedy notching Albion's equaliser five minutes before the final whistle.

SATURDAY 3rd FEBRUARY 1962

Albion lost 3-1 at Anfield in this second division fixture. Liverpool goalscorers include Roger Hunt and Ian St John. Up front for the Reds was future Seagulls boss Jimmy Melia. The club has played 12 competitive fixtures on this date since 1901. Only two have been away from home and five have resulted in Goldstone draws.

SATURDAY 4th FEBRUARY 1911

New banks of terracing on the east and north sides of the Goldstone Ground were in use for the first time for the visit of fellow Southern League side Coventry City in the FA Cup. A new record attendance of 13,000 witnessed a 0-0 draw.

THURSDAY 4th FEBRUARY 1937

Bobby Baxter was born in Yorkshire. The left-back was converted from a striker – 30 goals in 67 games – on signing from Bury in August 1961.

FRIDAY 4th FEBRUARY 1949

Brian 'Nobby' Horton was born in Hednesford. The inspirational midfielder – renowned for his non-stop chatter during matches – moved south after six seasons with Port Vale and captained his side to the first division in 1979. Nobby moved into management and has occupied the hotseat at Hull City, Oxford United, Manchester City, Huddersfield Town, Albion, Port Vale and Macclesfield Town.

SATURDAY 4th FEBRUARY 1950

Albion's reserves played in front of a 30,000 crowd at Highbury! The vast majority of those present were there to claim a ticket for Arsenal's forthcoming FA Cup fifth round tie with Burnley. The Gunners won the Football Combination Cup game 2-1.

TUESDAY 5th FEBRUARY 1901

Albion legend Tommy Cook was born in Cuckfield. The greatest goalscorer in the club's history – 123 in 209 starts – the centre-forward signed as an amateur in 1921 after leaving Southdown bus company. He topped the leading scorer charts in three seasons and led the England attack against Wales in 1925 as a third division player. An outstanding cricketer too, Tommy made 20,198 runs for his county between 1922 and 1937. Tragically, the great man took his own life in 1950 after failing to fully recover from a plane crash in which he was the only survivor.

SATURDAY 5th FEBRUARY 1910

Albion's second string played Norwich City at the Goldstone Ground. The Canaries' centre-half, Henrie Reid, left the pitch unwell and died of heart failure in the dressing-room.

SATURDAY 5th FEBRUARY 1985

Manager Chris Cattlin revealed he made a firm enquiry for St. Mirren striker Frank McAvennie but the asking price was too high… 'Brighton's money must be spent wisely and I will ensure that happens'. Next season, the bleached-blond Scottish hitman netted 26 goals for West Ham in the first division.

SATURDAY 6th FEBRUARY 1982

Everton were the Goldstone visitors for this first division fixture. Tony Grealish, Gerry Ryan and Steve Foster all registered to give Albion all three points – the first season of the new system – in a 3-1 victory that moved the Seagulls into UEFA Cup contention in eighth place.

SATURDAY 6th FEBRUARY 1988

Jack Shaw of Blackpool was so taken by Albion's away support at Bloomfield Road for the 3-1 victory he felt compelled to write into the programme: 'I was impressed with your travelling fans… especially when they are as well behaved as yours'.

WEDNESDAY 6th FEBRUARY 1991

Striker John Byrne marked his solitary international appearance for the Republic of Ireland while with Albion with a goal in the 3-0 victory over Wales in Wrexham.

SATURDAY 7th FEBRUARY 1903

The 1-1 Southern League second division draw at Wycombe Wanderers was the last first-team meeting between the clubs for more than 91 years.

THURSDAY 7th FEBRUARY 1929

One of Albion's all-time greats, Jimmy Langley, was born in Kilburn, London. The left-back signed from Leeds United in 1953. Immensely popular, Jimmy moved to Fulham for £12,000 in 1957 and earned full England honours a year later. The avid cigarette card collector was deeply superstitious and had to tap the left-hand post with each boot prior to kick-off in every game.

SATURDAY 7th FEBRUARY 1987

The natives were restless after the poor 3-0 home defeat to fellow second division strugglers Sunderland. Demonstrations inside the Goldstone Ground and in Newtown Road after the game called for chairman Bryan Bedson's head.

WEDNESDAY 8th FEBRUARY 1984

Former Albion left-back Gary Williams enjoyed a visit from his old team-mates to help promote his TV and video shop in Kemptown.

MONDAY 8th FEBRUARY 1988

Steve Gatting and Gerry Armstrong scored in the 3-2 defeat to Southampton in a five-a-side exhibition match during the 11th annual Sussex County League tournament at the Brighton Centre.

SATURDAY 8th FEBRUARY 1997

A very special day in the history of Brighton & Hove Football Club. Albion fans had been protesting all season. The internet was in its infancy and North Stand Chat was the place for fans to discuss ideas and all things Albion. Plymouth Argyle supporter Richard Vaughan suggested fans from every club in the league should lend their support and call for Archer and Bellotti to leave by turning up for the Hartlepool United game. Fans United was born. The rain and mist didn't dampen the remarkable scenes: fans from clubs around the world roared the Albion to a 5-0 victory. The result helped save the club from relegation to the Conference and possible oblivion.

Saturday 9th February 1946

The FA Cup returned after six years of war. Albion's first big game of the post-war era was against first division Derby County in the fifth round. The crowd of 23,456 was the biggest for 12 years. Unfortunately, the eventual Cup winners went home happy with a 4-1 first leg win. and won the return 6-0.

Saturday 9th February 1980

Something positive did come out of Albion's 5-1 first division thrashing at Southampton; Neil McNab made the first of 115 appearances in Brighton colours. The fiery Scot played as a 15-year-old for his local side, Greenock Morton, and was once suspended for pushing the referee at Carrow Road.

Saturday 9th February 1985

Cardiff City were the Goldstone visitors on this freezing afternoon. Defender Chris Hutchings took away some of the chill with the only goal of the game.

Saturday 10th February 1923

Albion's 2-1 third division (south) victory at Watford was not only the start of a four-game winning streak but also marked the debut of young Ulsterman Jimmy Hopkins. The inside-left had an exceptional turn of speed and arrived on the south coast after two seasons at Arsenal. A excellent return of 75 goals from 233 games ensures a permanent place in Albion's hall of fame.

Saturday 10th February 1973

A shocking run of 13 consecutive defeats thankfully came to an end at the Goldstone Ground. The 2-0 win over Luton Town was courtesy of a brace from Ken Beamish – and also saw the introduction of local-born youngster Tony Towner to the Hove faithful. The tricky winger netted on 25 occasions in his 183 appearances over seven seasons and was sold to Millwall for £65,000 in 1978 when Gerry Ryan arrived at the club.

Saturday 10th February 2001

Bobby Zamora's Withdean winner against promotion rivals Cardiff City took Albion a step nearer promotion from the bottom division.

SATURDAY 11th FEBRUARY 1905

Because of an impending FA Cup replay, Fulham postponed their reserve fixture with Albion at Craven Cottage and instead sent their second XI to the Goldstone for the Southern League first division match on the same day. The Cottagers were fined £20 for postponing the reserve match and £20 for fielding their second string at Hove. Fulham reserves won 4-1! The game was never replayed.

SATURDAY 11th FEBRUARY 1967

A crowd of 22,256 was at the Goldstone to see Albion v Notts County in a reserve fixture! Tickets were on sale for the FA Cup visit of high-flying Chelsea the next weekend. Around 15,000 fans stayed for the match.

SATURDAY 11th FEBRUARY 1978

Pop group Slade made a video in front of a packed North Stand for their single 'Give Us a Goal' before the 2-1 win over Burnley.

MONDAY 11th FEBRUARY 2002

Despite the greasy surface and incessant rain, Albion turned on the style in a top-of-the-table second division clash with Reading. Bobby Zamora opened the scoring (58) after a sublime back-heel from Paul Brooker. Steve Melton made it two with a brilliant volley 60 seconds later before Junior Lewis, on his full debut, slid in the third – 3-1.

SATURDAY 12th FEBRUARY 1966

In manager Archie Macaulay's programme notes against Scunthorpe United, the Scot recorded his pleasure in 'noting my request to supporters to refrain from throwing toilet rolls on to the pitch during play has been acted upon'.

SATURDAY 12th FEBRUARY 1983

Michael Robinson made his 100th first division appearance for Albion in the 0-0 draw with West Bromwich Albion. Graham Pearce listed bird watching of 'the feathered kind' as his hobby in the programme.

SATURDAY 12th FEBRUARY 2000

Bobby Zamora marked his loan debut from Bristol Rovers with Albion's only goal in a Withdean Stadium draw with Plymouth Argyle.

WEDNESDAY 13th FEBRUARY 1907

An unusual incident influenced the result along the coast. Albion were playing Hastings & St Leonards United when Julius Gregory, the left-back, was injured. As there were no substitutes in those days, Hugh MacDonald – the Albion goalkeeper – somewhat bizarrely came out of goal to take Gregory's place. With no-one between the sticks, Albion unsurprisingly lost the game 6-1!

SATURDAY 13th FEBRUARY 1965

Long-serving *Evening Argus* reporter John Vinicombe, recalling a memorable trip back from a 1-0 victory at Torquay on this day, wrote: 'Archie (the manager), well-pleased, ordered drinks all round with sumptuous dinner after which the coach set out for Brighton. One stop was followed by another, and another, and another. To say that staff and players of Brighton & Hove Albion were sloshed would be an understatement. We were all very nearly paralysed.'

SUNDAY 14th FEBRUARY 1971

Albion fans organised a walk along Brighton seafront in support of Pat Saward's 'Buy-a-Player' fund. The initiative raised around £1,500 which went towards the eventual purchase of Bert Murray, the 'People's Player', from Birmingham City.

SATURDAY 14th FEBRUARY 1987

Brighton-born Ian Chapman became Albion's youngest-ever player. The left-back replaced Chris Hutchings for the second division trip to Birmingham City. The tenacious defender packed a cracking shot. After 16 goals in 331 appearances, 'Chappers' was surprisingly released by manager Jimmy Case in 1996 and joined Gillingham.

SATURDAY 14th FEBRUARY 1998

There was plenty of love on the terraces as Albion faced Doncaster Rovers at Gillingham's Priestfield. The game was billed as 'Fans United 2 – The Heart of Football' to help highlight the joint plight of Albion and the Yorkshire outfit; they were rooted to the foot of the league after being ripped off by an unscrupulous chairman. An absolutely shocking game of football ensued and no-one in the 6,339 crowd – over 4,000 up on the average – was surprised to see a 0-0 draw.

SATURDAY 15th FEBRUARY 1986

fourth division Peterborough United hosted second division Albion in this FA Cup fifth round tie. Albion had only Graham Pearce left from the defeated 1983 Cup Final side. On a snowy day Steve Jacobs fired the orange ball home to make it 2-2 and send the 5,000-plus Albion fans among the 15,812 crowd back to Sussex looking forward to a replay…

SATURDAY 15th FEBRUARY 1997

A 2-1 third division defeat at Carlisle United will only be remembered for one reason: Hereford hero Robbie Reinelt made his debut…

SATURDAY 15th FEBRUARY 2003

Most of Albion's fans in the Centenary Stand at Valley Parade couldn't see Bobby Zamora net the winner in this first division fixture.

SATURDAY 16th FEBRUARY 1924

Jack Jenkins made his Wales debut in a 2-0 Home Championship defeat in Scotland. The full-back made his Football League bow after his 30th birthday and went on to represent the Albion for seven seasons, notching up 231 starts and four goals.

SATURDAY 16th FEBRUARY 1962

The Goldstone Ground saw its first postponement in the hardest winter for years. While other clubs had fixture after fixture cancelled, Albion managed to keep playing at home until the game against Watford was called off, ironically, due to a waterlogged pitch following the first thaw since the snows arrived on Boxing Day.

MONDAY 16th FEBRUARY 1970

Albion's last visit to Barrow's Holker Street ended in a 1-1 third division draw. Two years later the Cumbrian club were voted out of the Football League in favour of Hereford United.

SATURDAY 16th FEBRUARY 1980

The Goldstone hosted the battle of the Albions. A crowd of 22,633 watched the goalless draw against a strong West Bromwich side. It turned out to be the start of a run of six consecutive draws for Alan Mullery's side – a club record.

TUESDAY 17th FEBRUARY 1976

Peter Taylor decided on an ultra-defensive formation at Southend United in an attempt to end the dismal away form. The club's third division promotion challenge was suffering so the manager opted for four central defenders: Dennis Burnett, Andy Rollings, Graham Winstanley and Steve Piper. It failed spectacularly; Albion lost 4-0!

SATURDAY 17th FEBRUARY 1990

Albion moved up three places in the table – from 22nd to 19th – after Kevin Bremner's solitary first-half goal earned a victory over Leicester City in a second division game at the Goldstone.

SATURDAY 17th FEBRUARY 2007

Twice European Champions Nottingham Forest were the Withdean visitors. Quickfire goals from Dean Hammond (72 minutes) and Nick Ward (73) gave the Albion a 2-1 League One victory.

SATURDAY 18th FEBRUARY 1967

first division Chelsea were the guests for this FA Cup fourth round tie. A 35,000 sell-out Goldstone crowd witnessed a 1-1 draw with Dave Turner netting for Albion. The London club's flamboyant boss Tommy Docherty had this to say in the programme: 'They have a first division set-up at the Goldstone Ground, and first division ideas, as well as a first-class pitch. The day cannot be far away when they become one of our top clubs'. Meanwhile, on page 13, Turner – at 22 the club's youngest ever captain at the time – recalls how he 'fell off the settee' when he heard the Cup draw.

SATURDAY 18th FEBRUARY 1984

Southern Sound reported on their first Albion away game, the 3-1 FA Cup fifth round defeat at Watford's Vicarage Road.

WEDNESDAY 18th FEBRUARY 1987

Flying winger Steve Penney scored his first goal for Northern Ireland's in his country's 1-1 draw with Israel in Tel Aviv. On the same day, in Swansea, Dean Saunders represented his country for the fifth and final time as an Albion player in the 0-0 draw with the USSR before his £60,000 transfer to Oxford United.

SATURDAY 19th FEBRUARY 1972

It was goalless after 45 minutes at Gay Meadow. The floodgates opened for the second period as Albion ran out 5-3 winners with strikes from Peter O'Sullivan (2), Kit Napier and Willie Irvine, plus an own goal. The 1971/72 campaign produced the club's best-ever away record in the league: 12 wins and just five defeats, scoring 43 goals.

SATURDAY 19th FEBRUARY 1949

The East Terrace was inaugurated in a third division (south) match against promotion rivals Bournemouth & Boscombe Athletic. Don Welsh's Albion team ruined the celebrations by capitulating 6-1 to their south coast counterparts.

SUNDAY 19th FEBRUARY 1961

Justin Fashanu was born in Hackney, London. After a stunning goal against Liverpool, the Norwich City striker moved to Nottingham Forest in 1981. A fall-out with Brian Clough precipitated a move to Notts County – after a nine-game loan spell at Southampton – before £115,000 was paid for his services in 1985 by Chris Cattlin. The troubled striker managed just two strikes in 20 Albion run-outs and spent the next 12 years plying his trade at various club across Europe and North America. Tragically, Justin took his own life in May 1998.

SATURDAY 20th FEBRUARY 1982

Albion fans looked on all misty-eyed as Peter Ward scored for Nottingham Forest in the 1-0 first division defeat at the Goldstone.

SUNDAY 20th FEBRUARY 1983

FA Cup victories over Newcastle United and Manchester City were rewarded with a fifth round tie at league champions Liverpool! No team had won at Anfield for almost a year, while the Reds hadn't lost a home cup tie since 1964. Albion had been victorious on the road only once all season – at St. James' Park in the third round. Amazingly, Gerry Ryan put the Seagulls ahead just after the half hour. Australian Craig Johnston equalised with an acrobatic strike with 20 minutes remaining only for former Kop favourite Jimmy Case to blast home the winner from 20 yards sixty seconds later. Phil Neal missed a penalty and Albion were in the last eight.

SATURDAY 21st FEBRUARY 1914

Albion, cheered on by around 400 travelling fans, bowed out of the FA Cup at the third round stage, losing 3-0 to The Wednesday in Sheffield. The Owls – who were once known as the Blades before relocating to the north of the city – were so impressed by the performance of Albion's centre-half David Parkes that they offered a fee of £1,500 plus forward George Beech for the promising 21-year-old: Parkes subsequently moved to Yorkshire for a then-record sum for an Albion player.

SATURDAY 21st FEBRUARY 1953

Keeper Eric Gill made the first of 247 consecutive appearances and got off to a great start, keeping a clean sheet at Reading's Elm Park.

SUNDAY 21st FEBRUARY 1982

The first-team squad and coaching staff flew to Torremolinos, in Spain, for a short break and a spot of golf.

SATURDAY 22nd FEBRUARY 1902

The Albion played their first-ever game at the Goldstone Ground, Newtown Road, Hove, as a Sussex Senior Cup semi-final was taking place at the County Ground, the club's home pitch. The opponents for the historic friendly were Southampton Wanderers, who were soundly beaten 7-1. The club moved permanently to the Goldstone for 1902/03 and became the sole occupants in 1904.

WEDNESDAY 22nd FEBRUARY 1967

After a 1-1 FA Cup fourth round result at the Goldstone, Albion faced a replay with Chelsea at Stamford Bridge. Around 1,000 Albion fans were locked out but 54,852 spectators witnessed the 4-0 defeat.

SATURDAY 22nd FEBRUARY 1969

Alex Dawson – a big, powerful centre-forward and once a Busby Babe at Manchester United – scored four times at Hartlepool in a 5-2 Albion third division win: a fourth successive victory.

SATURDAY 22nd FEBRUARY 2003

Super-sub Tony Rougier immediately endeared himself to the Withdean faithful with the only goal on his debut versus Millwall.

SATURDAY 23rd FEBRUARY 1924

After humbling the mighty Everton 5-2 in the second round, Manchester City visited the Goldstone Ground. Five goals appeared on the scoresheet again but, unfortunately, it was the Sky Blues who progressed winning 5-1.

SATURDAY 23rd FEBRUARY 1963

A nine-goal bonanza surprised the 5,934 in attendance for a third division game at Elm Park. Reading were 2-1 up at the break but Albion fought back with efforts from Alan Jackson (2), Roy Jennings (2) and Steve Burtenshaw.

TUESDAY 23rd FEBRUARY 1982

Steve Foster shone on his debut in the centre of England's defence in the 4-0 Wembley demolition of Northern Ireland in a Home International: he becomes the first Albion player to wear the three lions since Tommy Cook in 1925. Club team-mate left-back Sammy Nelson lined up for the opposition.

SATURDAY 24th FEBRUARY 1976

It was a historic day in Hove. A bumper crowd of 33,300 – over 19,000 up on the visit of Halifax Town three days earlier – were at the Goldstone for the visit of arch rivals Crystal Palace for a third division fixture. Northern Ireland international Sammy Morgan's brace earnt a 2-0 victory for Peter Taylor's men but the day will be remembered for the first, en masse chant of "Seagulls", as a reply to the Croydon outfit's "Eagles" song.

TUESDAY 24th FEBRUARY 1981

Albion beat Southampton for the first time in 24 years. The first division encounter included a Gary Williams penalty and a strike from midfielder from Giles Stille. The result – in front of 23,715 fans – was the first win in eight games for Alan Mullery's side.

SATURDAY 24th FEBRUARY 1990

Sergei Gotsmanov made his debut in the 2-1 second division defeat at Sunderland. The midfielder scored four times in 16 appearances before being transferred to Southampton for £150,000 six months later.

Saturday 25th February 1911

Don Welsh was born in Manchester. After playing for Valletta in Malta while in the Navy, the half-back joined Torquay United. Charlton Athletic paid £3,250 for his services and the left-sided player helped them win the FA Cup in 1947. Just six months later Welsh took over the Albion hotseat from Tommy Cook before leaving for Liverpool in March 1951.

Wednesday 25th February 1970

Albion played Walsall at West Bromwich Albion's Hawthorns in this third division fixture; Fellows Park had been waterlogged for some weeks. Dave Turner (2) and Kit Napier were the scorers in a 3-0 win.

Wednesday 26th February 1958

Major Carlo Campbell died aged 70 at the Sussex County Hospital. A fighter pilot in World War I, the Albion chairman – held in high esteem across the country – had been advised to slow down by his doctors. His deputy, Alec Whitcher, told the Brighton & Hove Herald; 'The major's death is a grievous blow to us all'.

Saturday 26th February 1977

Peter Grummitt kept his fifth successive clean sheet in the 1-0 third division win at York City.

Thursday 26th February 1998

Albion midfield legend Brian Horton began his 11-month tenure as Brighton boss. A good start – a 3-2 home (Gillingham) win over Chester City – gave false hope and only one further win was registered on the way to a 23rd-place finish. The following campaign showed improvement but Horton moved to Port Vale in January 1999.

Saturday 26th February 2000

Albion went goal crazy at the Deva Stadium to relieve the pressure on manager Micky Adams. Bobby Zamora grabbed a quick-fire brace within the first 20 minutes. The floodgates opened in the second half as Keith McPherson, Paul Brooker, Zamora (pen), Darren Freeman and Paul Rogers also score in a stunning 7-1 win for Albion! The win started an unbeaten run through to the end of the season.

FRIDAY 27th FEBRUARY 1903

The Evening Argus proudly proclaimed that 'the Brighton & Hove Albion management have been successful in inducing Woolwich Arsenal to visit Brighton [for a friendly]... the club should be congratulated on their enterprise'.

SATURDAY 27th FEBRUARY 1974

'The People's Player', Bert Murray, made his debut in the 2-1 third division victory over Wrexham. The utility player was on the verge of signing for Fulham when manager Pat Saward stepped in to sign the Chelsea League Cup winner. The following season Bert was instrumental in the exciting promotion charge, scoring 12 times, and was voted 'Player of the Season'.

SATURDAY 27th FEBRUARY 1982

The club announced they are trying to attract fans to splash out on the new executive boxes that would be built as part of the Goldstone's new North Stand. The proposed development never happened.

WEDNESDAY 27th FEBRUARY 1991

A group of Albion fans departed Newtown Road for a midweek fixture at Newcastle United. The coach made a comfort stop at Toddington services for food and refreshments. Before continuing the long journey north, police instructed the vehicle to pull over and ordered the bemused fans to disembark. The car park area was cleared and it was nearly three hours before everyone could move on. It transpired that Chelsea fans on their way to Sheffield Wednesday telephoned police with a hoax bomb call. The coach arrived at St. James' Park with 10 minutes to spare, but the misery didn't end there. The fans got soaked to the skin on an uncovered terrace, as they endured a painfully dull 0-0 draw. The attendance was just 12,692.

SATURDAY 27th FEBRUARY 1993

Kurt Nogan's hot streak was about to start. Unfortunately, only 2,033 people witnessed the striker's brace at Wigan Athletic's Springfield Park. The former Luton man scored 15 times in the last 18 games of the season to become the first player since Garry Nelson five years earlier to net more than 20 league goals in a campaign.

SATURDAY 28th FEBRUARY 1903

Frank Scott scored five in an 8-0 mauling of Southall in this Southern League Division Two fixture in west London.

SATURDAY 28th FEBRUARY 1925

Tommy Cook represented England for the one and only time in the 2-1 Home Championship victory over Wales in Swansea.

SATURDAY 28th FEBRUARY 1953

A huge crowd of 10,000 fans turned up at the Goldstone for a reserve fixture with Spurs, in the Football Combination Cup. The first team drew 3-3 at Queens Park Rangers in a third division (south) match.

SATURDAY 28th FEBRUARY 1998

Brian Horton returned for his first game in charge, against Chester City at Gillingham. A strike from Andy Ansah and a brace by Kerry Mayo handed the new boss a 3-2 victory.

SATURDAY 28th FEBRUARY 2004

Adam Virgo scored his first Albion goal in the second division 1-1 draw at Stockport County's Edgeley Park.

SATURDAY 29th FEBRUARY 1908

Dundonians Dave Dougal and Tom Rodger both made their Southern League debuts in the 1-0 home defeat to Crystal Palace.

SATURDAY 29th FEBRUARY 1936

Alec Law grabbed both goals in the 2-1 third division (south) victory at Gillingham.

SATURDAY 29th FEBRUARY 1964

Gillingham visited the Goldstone for a fourth division encounter. In front of 15,349, Jimmy Collins and Jack Smith scored in a 2-1 win.

SATURDAY 29th FEBRUARY 1992

Raphael Meade, Robert Codner, and Stuart Munday sealed a 3-2 second division victory over Southend United. Despite the Goldstone triumph, the Seagulls are still bottom of the table.

Brighton & Hove Albion
ON THIS DAY

MARCH

Thursday 1st March 1951

Schoolboy high-jump and 800 metres champion Gerry Fell was born in Nottinghamshire. Signed by Peter Taylor in 1974, the unusually tall winger possessed electric pace and a powerful shot and would go on to net 20 times in 91 Albion appearances before departing for Southend United in 1977 as part of the deal that bought Paul Clark to the club.

Saturday 1st March 1958

Dave Hollins, brother of Chelsea star John, wore the Albion goalkeeping jersey for the first time in the 2-2 draw at Coventry City. The Welshman moved to Newcastle United for £11,000 in 1961.

Tuesday 1st March 1983

Despite reaching the FA Cup Final in this season, Albion only managed one league victory on the road. Michael Robinson and Jimmy Case scored the goals in a 2-1 triumph at fellow strugglers Swansea City.

Saturday 2nd March 1912

Jimmy Smith scored three in the 7-1 Southern League Division One demolition of Watford at the Goldstone. The diminutive forward established a new record of 25 league goals in his first full season and managed 40 overall in just 65 games. Eight months later he was sold for £735 (plus Bobby Simpson) to Bradford (Park Avenue), but was tragically killed in action on the Western Front in 1918.

Saturday 2nd March 1957

Goalkeeper Eric Gill had made 247 consecutive appearances – 231 in the league and 16 in the FA Cup – and at Coventry was due to break the record held by Tottenham Hotspur's Ted Ditchburn. Unfortunately, the £400 signing from Charlton Athletic felt unwell and was sent home from Brighton station. Billy Lane's men wore an unusual change strip of black shirts with white sleeves.

Tuesday 2nd March 1982

Steve Foster was pictured in the club's official programme for the match with Leeds United with a huge blue and white toy kangaroo that Albion fan Niki Hassett sent from Australia.

SATURDAY 3rd MARCH 1970

A trip to the seaside saw Albion's 12-game unbeaten run ended. A 2-0 defeat to Southport at Haig Avenue puts paid to a sequence that saw 17 goals scored and just three conceded.

MONDAY 3rd MARCH 1986

Four hundred helpful Albion fans cleared the Goldstone pitch and terraces of snow and were rewarded with free entry to the FA Cup fifth round replay against Peterborough United. Dean Saunders net the only goal in front of 19,010 fans.

SATURDAY 3rd MARCH 1990

Barry Lloyd saw the future success of the Albion's Football in the Community initiative: "Here in Sussex our community covers many hundreds of square miles, we can confidently look forwards to the time when we have one of the most successful schemes in the country."

FRIDAY 4th MARCH 1921

Wilfred McCoy was born in Birmingham. Known by his nickname 'Tim' (after the famous cowboy) the big centre-half's career was interrupted by the war and he eventually made his peacetime debut in 1951, 11 years after his first wartime appearance at Portsmouth.

SATURDAY 4th MARCH 1972

The team coach failed to arrive at Albion's Manchester hotel so four taxis were required to ferry Pat Saward and his team to Halifax in the nick of time. The team were unaffected by the panic as Willie Irvine, Bert Murray, Kit Napier and John Templeman (2) hit the goals in a resounding 5-0 victory.

TUESDAY 4th MARCH 1997

Northampton Town were the victims of a Jason Peake thunderbolt in this 2-1 third division win. Albion sat at the bottom of the league.

SUNDAY 4th MARCH 2007

The club's community scheme won national acclaim as Albion in the Community won the Football League's FourFourTwo Community Club of the Year Award.

SATURDAY 5th MARCH 1927

The receipts from the 9,447 in attendance for a 3-2 third division (south) win over Gillingham went to Tommy Cook. Before the 1930s, long-serving players due a benefit were often rewarded with gate money from a league game rather than a separate testimonial match. Albion's record league goalscorer netted just over £437. The lowest admission price between the wars was one shilling.

SATURDAY 5th MARCH 1977

The 1-1 third division draw with Tranmere Rovers was marred by the injury sustained by Peter Grummitt – in a collision with visiting forward Ronnie Moore – which ended his professional career.

TUESDAY 5th MARCH 2002

Albion kept the pressure on second division leaders Reading with a 4-0 thumping of Wycombe Wanderers at Withdean. Bobby Zamora (2), Paul Brooker and Paul Watson (25-yard free-kick) were the scorers.

SATURDAY 6th MARCH 1982

Albion travelled to Anfield to face a mighty Liverpool side that included Ian Rush, Kenny Dalglish and Mark Lawrenson. Jimmy Case found himself wide on the right and sent over an inviting centre which Michael Robinson nodded across for Andy Ritchie to fire goalwards. Bruce Grobbelaar palmed the ball on to Alan Hansen's legs and over the line. The 1-0 win sent the Albion into eighth place in the first division.

SATURDAY 6th MARCH 1985

In the programme against Blackburn Rovers, Glen Wilson waxed lyrical about his time at the Albion: "To me, Brighton is the most wonderful club in the country. It's a great club, it always has been. We've got very good supporters and I think the club has always tried to remain close to the people who come along and support them. Every day I come to work here, is like a day going to Wembley. That's how attached I've become to the club".

WEDNESDAY 6th MARCH 1996

Kevin McGarrigle scored his only Albion goal in the 2-0 win at Wycombe's Adams Park.

MONDAY 7th MARCH 1910

Albion travelled to east London for a Southern League fixture at Brisbane Road, but it wasn't against Orient. The O's were then known as Clapton Orient and played a few miles to the west. Albion drew 1-1 with hosts Leyton FC, who still exist as Leyton Pennant.

SATURDAY 7th MARCH 1981

Just under 15,000 Goldstone fans were present for 19-year-old Tony Vessey's one and only Albion run-out against Coventry City (who wore a brown kit). The defender had a brief spell in Sweden before playing for Worthing and Crawley Town, where he made over 400 appearances.

SATURDAY 7th MARCH 1998

Albion drew 0-0 at Hartlepool's Victoria Park in a third division contest. Fast forward two years, to the day, and Albion drew 0-0 at Hartlepool's Victoria Park – in the third division!

SATURDAY 8th MARCH 1986

first division Southampton were the visitors to the Goldstone Ground a sixth round FA Cup tie. It was only the Albion's second ever appearance at this stage of the FA Cup and the 25,069 fans present were hoping for an upset against a side that included four England internationals. Saints overwhelmed their hosts to win 2-0.

SATURDAY 8th MARCH 1997

In an incident-packed campaign, most of the action was taking place off the pitch. Not this time, though, as Leyton Orient visited the Goldstone Ground. A real humdinger of a contest exploded into life as Craig Maskell scored twice in the first seven minutes. Unbelievably, Orient were 3-2 up by the hour mark. Ian Baird then equalised only for Scott McGleish to fire the Londoners into the lead again and celebrate wildly in front of the North Stand – much to the annoyance of the home crowd. That was followed by a pitch invasion by three supporters, one of whom attempted to attack the referee, but was stopped by former England international Ray Wilkins. O's defender Mark Warren was sent off to add to the drama before Scottish winger Paul McDonald levelled from the spot with five minutes remaining to make it 4-4. The point was vital come the end of the season as Albion stayed up on goals scored.

SATURDAY 9th MARCH 1957

Albion thrashed Northampton Town 5-0 at the Goldstone. Albert Mundy (2), Denis Foreman and Peter Harburn (2) settled the third division (south) contest in front of 11,922 supporters. This date has been particularly jinxed since Albion's league debut in 1920. Only one win and two draws have been recorded in 11 games.

WEDNESDAY 9th MARCH 1988

Albion were chasing promotion, but also had Wembley in their sights – in the Sherpa Van Trophy. The visit of Notts County attracted a healthy crowd of 8,499 but the result didn't match the fans' enthusiasm as Albion lost 5-1 at the Goldstone.

SATURDAY 9th MARCH 2002

An entertaining encounter at the Madejski Stadium saw two promotion contenders play out a 0-0 draw. Albion wide man Gary Hart fired in an angled drive in front of the ecstatic travelling army in the final minute. Referee Mike Dean disallowed the strike.

SATURDAY 10th MARCH 1928

Ernie 'Tug' Wilson enjoyed the first of two benefit matches. The record appearance holder – 566 games – netted just over £326 from the third division (south) game against Gillingham at the Goldstone. The 7,860 spectators did not see any goals.

SATURDAY 10th MARCH 1951

A 2-2 draw at Bournemouth & Boscombe Athletic was the first game of Billy Lane's ten-year spell as boss. The former Spurs striker – who scored 177 goals for seven clubs – joined as Don Welsh's assistant in 1950. On taking charge he brought back blue and white stripes. Lane, who changed his surname from Lohn during World War I because of its German association, oversaw the club's first league promotion in 1958.

SUNDAY 10th MARCH 1974

Power cuts brought the country to its knees. Albion – to try and increase gate revenue – hosted only their second-ever Sunday match. It worked as 17,061 fans saw the 2-1 win over Hereford United. The season's average was 10,848.

SATURDAY 11th MARCH 1950

Cyril Thompson embarked on a year-long Albion career scoring in the 4-2 defeat at Notts County. The forward netted 16 times, including eight goals in successive league games – a club record – in October 1950.

MONDAY 11th MARCH 1974

In Epping, Essex, a hero was born and named Robbie Reinelt. The journeyman striker cost Albion £15,000 from Colchester United in February 1997. An inauspicious start – two goals in 11 games – and Reinelt found himself on the bench for the end-of-season nail-biter at Hereford on 3rd May 1997…

SATURDAY 12th MARCH 1960

Bill Curry scored one of his three hat-tricks for the season in the 5-1 second division win over Bristol City at the Goldstone Ground.

SATURDAY 12th MARCH 1983

The Goldstone Ground was full to its 28,000 capacity for the visit of Norwich City in the FA Cup sixth round. It was the furthest the Albion had ever progressed in the competition and the excitement in the twin towns was almost at fever pitch! Jimmy Case had netted in the previous three rounds and it was the Scouser who fired the Albion to a semi-final date with Sheffield Wednesday at Highbury. Andy Ritchie flicked on for the midfielder who muscled through the Canaries' defence to slot past future England keeper Chris Woods in front of an ecstatic North Stand. Wembley beware, the Seagulls are on their way…

THURSDAY 12th MARCH 1987

Dean Saunders – who would go on to be transferred for over £10m in total, score 185 goals in 559 league appearances and net 22 times in 75 international matches for Wales – was sold for a paltry £60,000 to Oxford United on the insistence of the club's directors.

TUESDAY 12th MARCH 1997

Good news from London. At the offices of the Centre for Dispute Resolution, director Greg Stanley told the press that a deal had been struck between himself and Bill Archer, and the consortium led by Dick Knight. It was another six months before the deal was completed.

SATURDAY 13th MARCH 1954

Albion enjoyed a 3-0 third division (south) home win over Crystal Palace. Bert Addinall, Frankie Howard and Dennis Gordon scored the goals. The win put Albion three points ahead of Ipswich Town at the top as Billy Lane's men chased the club's first promotion since joining the Football League.

MONDAY 13th MARCH 1978

The Brighton Trades & Labour Club – in Lewes Road, Brighton – hosted the first-ever Seagull Lottery draw. In the early days the 50,000 20p tickets quickly sold out each week and there was even a waiting list! The draw was made in pubs across Sussex until 1991.

WEDNESDAY 13th MARCH 1985

The mulleted Alan Biley got his first Albion run-out in the goalless draw at Barnsley. Much-loved by Portsmouth fans – he scored 51 times in 101 games – Biley was sold by Alan Ball for just £50,000. Having commanded two transfer fees over £300,000 – to Everton and Derby County respectively – the striker managed only nine goals in 40 appearances and moved abroad in May 1987.

SATURDAY 14th MARCH 1925

Inside-right Sam Jennings made his debut in the 1-0 defeat at Northampton Town. Manager Charlie Webb paid a club record fee of £650 to West Ham United and the Nottinghamshire-born hitman didn't disappoint, scoring 63 goals in just 115 starts.

SATURDAY 14th MARCH 1990

Sheffield United's 1989/90 team photo in the programme featured many future Albion connections: Bob Booker (assistant manager and caretaker boss (twice) 2001 to 2006); Chris Wilder (player 1999); Mark Morris (player 1996/97) and Darren Carr (player 1999/00).

SATURDAY 14th MARCH 1998

In what proved to be one of the Albion's worst-ever seasons in 1997/98, striker Damien Hilton played his first of four goalless games in the 0-0 basement draw at Barnet.

MONDAY 15th MARCH 1909

Charlie Webb became the first Albion player to represent his country. The inside-left featured for the Republic of Ireland in the 5-0 defeat against Scotland in Glasgow.

SATURDAY 15th MARCH 1980

After playing Manchester United for the first time in Sussex – a Goldstone Ground 0-0 stalemate (the sixth draw in a row) – Peter Ward and his wife were among a panel of fashion competition judges at Butlins Ocean Hotel in Saltdean, alongside pop sensations Dollar.

TUESDAY 15th MARCH 2005

Premiership-bound Wigan Athletic gave Albion a football masterclass in a Championship encounter at Withdean. The Latics were 4-0 up after 34 minutes in front of 6,306 gobsmacked fans. Adam Virgo and Dean Hammond added a hint of respectability to the 4-2 scoreline.

THURSDAY 16th MARCH 1905

An extraordinary meeting of Albion shareholders was called at the Presbyterian Lecture Hall in North Road, Brighton. The directors in attendance agreed to purchase 750 shares to fund the players' summer wages. It was announced that John Jackson was to be replaced by respected Middlesex Football administrator Frank Scott-Walford due to his poor bookkeeping which he'd neglected for four months, leaving the club's finances in a mess.

SATURDAY 16th MARCH 1996

A low Goldstone Ground crowd of just 4,910 witnessed Craig Maskell's first two goals for Albion in a 4-0 win over Hull City.

SATURDAY 16th MARCH 1991

In the matchday programme versus Blackburn Rovers it's announced that Albion had won the 1991 Rothmans Football League Commercial Managers' Bursary for the most innovative and successful commercial campaign in all four divisions. Marketing manager Terry Gill initiated the launch of Sports Express, Albion's very own kit supplier. A notable shirt was the red-and-white small-checked away number that looked pink from afar.

FRIDAY 17th MARCH 1967

Brian Dear – who once scored five goals in 20 minutes for West Ham – made the first of only seven appearances on loan from the Upton Park outfit. The club's first player signed in such a deal, the Plaistow-born inside-forward scored five times during his Goldstone stay but a £20,000 price tag was deemed too expensive.

SATURDAY 17th MARCH 1973

Ken Beamish's strike earned Albion a draw against Sheffield Wednesday at Hillsborough. It was the first point for Pat Saward's team away from the Goldstone for nearly five months.

THURSDAY 17th MARCH 1983

Genial Liverpudlian Jimmy Melia was appointed Albion manager.

SATURDAY 17th MARCH 1984

Albion triumphed over Derby at the Goldstone. Perry Digweed returned in goal – his first game since Joe Corrigan's arrival six months earlier – and kept a clean sheet in the 3-0 second division win. Gordon Smith netted in his final game before his move to Manchester City.

WEDNESDAY 18th MARCH 1908

Goals from Jack Hall, Bert Longstaff and Arthur Hulme earned Albion a 3-2 win over Southampton in the Southern League's first division in front of around 2,000 fans.

SATURDAY 18th MARCH 1911

Charlie Webb made his third and final appearance for Ireland in the same place he made his debut, Glasgow.

TUESDAY 18th MARCH 1986

Blackburn Rovers entertained Albion at Ewood Park. A gate of just 3,616 watched the visitors tear apart the home side. Terry Connor, Danny Wilson (2), and Dean Saunders scored in a 4-1 win.

SATURDAY 18th MARCH 1995

Nicky Rust's run of five consecutive third division clean sheets is ended in the 1-0 loss at York City.

Saturday 19th March 1932

Ernest 'Ernie' King made his debut in the 3-0 defeat at Fulham in the third division (south). The full-back, a sliding tackle expert, made 217 appearances without scoring.

Saturday 19th March 1983

Steve Gatting scored Albion's goal at Manchester United. The 1-1 first division draw in front of 36,700 Old Trafford fans proved to be former United starlet Andy Ritchie's final game before being swapped for Leeds United's Terry Connor in a deal rated at £500,000.

Saturday 19th March 1988

Gary Chivers joined Albion in a £40,000 deal from Watford. The popular defender began his career with Chelsea and, after making 252 appearances and scoring 16 times, moved to Bournemouth in 1993.

Saturday 20th March 1926

Albion won 1-0 at Merthyr Town in the Division Three (South). The victory is the club's third win on the road in the last four games. Goalscorer Sam Jennings would go on to net 20 times that season.

Saturday 20th March 1976

The 2-0 Goldstone victory over Swindon Town was the Albion's 17th third division home win of the season in 20 league games.

Tuesday 20th March 1979

Two goals from Peter Ward earned Albion a 2-1 win over Bristol Rovers at Eastville and ensured top spot in Division Two is maintained.

Wednesday 20th March 1991

Garry Nelson replaced the injured Mike Small in the team and grabbed a brace in the 2-0 Goldstone win over West Bromwich Albion. The win – in front of 6,676 fans – moved the Albion up two places to fifth.

Saturday 20th March 1999

Phil King, Lee Doherty, Duncan McArthur and Keith McPherson all made their Albion debuts in the 0-0 third division draw at Hartlepool. Only McPherson made any impact, going on to make 37 appearances.

Sunday 21st March 1965

Paul Rogers was born in Portsmouth. 'Dodge', as he is affectionately known by Albion fans, was a late starter. He joined Sheffield United from Sutton United as a 26-year-old in 1992 and represented Wigan Athletic and Notts County before settling in Sussex. Guaranteed a place in the history books, the former midfielder is best remembered for being club captain during the back-to-back championship triumphs of 2000/01 and 2001/02.

Saturday 21st March 1987

An Albion legend made his debut at Ipswich Town. John Crumplin began his Brighton career as a winger and a succession of below-par showings resulted in barracking by sections of the crowd. A move to right-back revitalised the Bath-born player and, with renewed confidence, he became the darling of the North Stand with some wholehearted performances. In 1990/91 Albion fanzine Gulls Eye released a 'football genius' T-shirt – initially meant to be ironic – that eventually became a collector's item.

Monday 21st March 2005

Reading won 1-0 at Withdean in the Championship. The visitors line-up included Ivar Ingimarsson, Steve Sidwell and goalscorer Nicky Forster. The latter joined Brighton from Hull City for a £75,000 in July 2007 and netted in a pre-season friendly at Worthing in his first appearance in an Albion shirt.

Saturday 22nd March 1958

Crystal Palace cruised into a two-goal lead in front of 19,517 fans at the Goldstone Ground. Denis Foreman grabbed one back on the hour before Dave Sexton equalised with ten minutes remaining. Manager Billy Lane headed down the tunnel just as the final seconds were ticking down. Big centre-forward Peter Harburn nicked the winner with just five seconds on the clock to cue a wild pitch invasion from the North Stand by celebrating fans.

Monday 22nd March 1982

Manager Mike Bailey and chairman Mike Bamber hosted an 'Albion Forum', sponsored by Whitbreads, at the Brighton Centre.

SATURDAY 23rd MARCH 1991

Albion beat Swindon Town 3-1 – with goals from Clive Walker, Robert Codner (pen) and Garry Nelson – at the County Ground, the third win in a row for Barry Lloyd's men. The result lifted the Seagulls up to fourth in Division Two.

FRIDAY 23rd MARCH 1973

Ian Goodwin scored the only goal in the Goldstone friendly win over Spartak Moscow. The Russians – who included five internationals in their line-up – played the Albion as a warm-up for their Cup Winners' Cup quarter-final against AC Milan.

SATURDAY 23rd MARCH 1955

Albion moved up to 11th in the third division (south) after a 5-3 home win over Exeter City. Just 4,175 fans turned up to see goals from Dennis Gordon, Bernard Moore, Albert Mundy (2) and Frankie Howard.

THURSDAY 24th MARCH 1881

William Jones was born in Staffordshire. 'Bullet' enjoyed two spells with the Albion – 1909-1912 and 1913-1920 – finding the target 69 times in 179 matches. The 5ft 5ins striker was incredibly popular in Hove and, on hanging up his boots, worked in a variety of roles at the Goldstone.

SATURDAY 24th MARCH 1962

A run of nine defeats wasn't ideal preparation for the visit of Walsall. Manager George Curtis made changes: in came in Bobby Laverick, Joe Carolan and Ian McNeill for Johnny Cochrane, Mike Tiddy and Bob McNicol. It worked as goals from Laverick (2) and Roy Jennings seal a 3-2 win. Albion remained bottom of the second division.

SATURDAY 24th MARCH 1973

Tricia Burtenshaw was crowned Miss Albion at the Supporters' Club dance at the Arlington Hotel in Brighton.

SATURDAY 24th MARCH 1984

A girls' soccer team from the USA adopted the Albion's name and colours. The Brighton Seagulls played in the Los Angeles District Junior League and had just won their league title.

SATURDAY 25th MARCH 1905

Albion enjoyed a 3-1 Goldstone win over West Ham United in the Southern League Division One. On picking himself up after putting his side 2-1 ahead, Bertie Lyon was kicked by the Hammers' England goalkeeper Matt Kingsley. The crowd spilled on to the pitch and swarmed around the West Ham players. Ugly scenes ensued and when order was restored, Kingsley was sent off and Lyon was carried to the dressing-room to receive treatment.

WEDNESDAY 25th MARCH 1903

W Ward – who had a better goals-to-game ratio than his namesake Peter, albeit in just three matches – scored a brace on his debut in the 9-1 thumping of Hitchin Town. In his final appearance, he notched a hat-trick in the South East League fixture versus Bedford Queen's Engineering Works.

FRIDAY 25th MARCH 1910

In the first of four games in just five days, Albion disposed of Exeter City in a 2-1 Southern League Division One win. The Brighton & Hove Herald reported that: 'the gate amounted to £338 and over 4,000 bicycles were housed during the game… Longstaff opened the scoring… needless to say, the great crowd cheered; the noise must have been heard miles away'.

SATURDAY 25th MARCH 1972

Pat Saward dropped skipper John Napier, in favour of Ian Goodwin, for the visit of third division leaders Aston Villa. Albion triumphed 2-1 with goals in either half from Willie Irvine and Kit Napier in front of 28,833 Goldstone fans. Irvine's superb strike was eventually voted a runner-up in the BBC's *Match of the Day* programme's Goal of the Season competition.

SATURDAY 25th MARCH 1989

"Football was very different in Saudi Arabia. In one match the keeper was lobbed by an attacker and his whole team dropped to their knees to pray. The ball bounced over the crossbar. They danced around in delight – personally I blamed it on the Astroturf," recalls former Albion midfielder Geoff Cooper in that day's match programme.

SATURDAY 26th MARCH 1910

The crowd were in hysterics as the referee was caught up in the action, receiving a swift kick to the knee. Mr Muir had to be on his toes at the beginning of the second half as Albion netted three times in four minutes against New Brompton in a 5-1 Goldstone victory.

WEDNESDAY 26th MARCH 1975

Albion beat AFC Bournemouth 2-1 at the Goldstone. The third division victory was the tenth consecutive home game on this date going back to 1932.

WEDNESDAY 26th MARCH 1980

In Nicosia, Mark Lawrenson scored for the Republic of Ireland in the 3-2 win against Cyprus in a World Cup qualifier.

WEDNESDAY 27th MARCH 1912

The Albion Supporters' Club was formed – one of the earliest in the country – by Harry Edwards.

SATURDAY 27th MARCH 1954

The first crowd of over 30,000 was at the Goldstone for a Football League match in the third division (south) against promotion rivals Southampton: 31,025 saw Bert Addinall and Dennis Gordon net in a 2-1 win. The result kept Albion three points clear at the top.

SATURDAY 27th MARCH 1965

Promising right-half Barrie Rees was tragically killed in a car crash while en route to his parents' home in Rhyl. The Welshman had arrived less than three months earlier from Everton and had already made a big impression among the fans. A sad day in the club's history.

SATURDAY 27th MARCH 1976

A memorable day in Albion folklore... manager Peter Taylor decided to bring in a slightly-built 20-year-old forward to replace leading scorer Fred Binney at league leaders Hereford United. After less than a minute of his first Albion appearance, Peter Ward netted. Hereford later equalised, but a legend is born...

SATURDAY 28th MARCH 1925

Albion moved up to ninth in the third division (south) table after thrashing Queens Park Rangers 5-0 at the Goldstone Ground in front of 6,500 fans. Albion legend Tommy Cook struck twice. Sam Jennings, Jack Smith and a penalty from Wally Little sealed the points.

SATURDAY 28th MARCH 1992

The Professional Footballers Association was frustrated by the potential 'Super League'. A strike was proposed to occur during the title run-ins.

TUESDAY 28th MARCH 1995

A pitifully low crowd of just 2,316 was present at Millmoor for Albion's Division Two visit. John Byrne and his namesake Paul (on loan from Celtic) were on the scoresheet, along with Stuart Myall. Unfortunately, Rotherham United scored four against Liam Brady's men.

SATURDAY 29th MARCH 1980

A Gary Williams strike gave the Albion a second 1-0 league victory over Nottingham Forest; the only club to do the double over the European Cup holders during the season. Before the match world middleweight champion Alan Minter was awarded with a tracksuit – in the club's new all blue colours for the following campaign and embroidered with his name – by chairman Mike Bamber.

FRIDAY 29th MARCH 1985

The attraction of the Grand National had affected crowds in previous years so Friday night football was played at the Goldstone for the first time, attracting a gate of 10,005. Alan Biley scored his first goal in Albion colours. Strike partner Terry Connor grabbed the other, in a 2-0 victory over Oldham Athletic.

SATURDAY 29th MARCH 1997

Despite a fantastic strike from Jeff Minton, Albion went down 2-1 at Chester City's Deva Stadium. Defeat left Steve Gritt's men four points behind Hereford United with just six games to play. Despised chairman Bill Archer was in attendance, but when asked by a fan when there might be an announcement on the mediation talks with Dick Knight his reply was: "What's it got to do with you?"

FRIDAY 30th MARCH 1962

One of only two Albion players to progress through the club's ranks to full England international honours – the other was Tommy Cook – Gary Stevens was born in Hillingdon, Middlesex. The versatile defender/midfielder was released by Ipswich Town in 1978 and arrived at the Goldstone as an apprentice. A reserve team place cemented, manager Alan Mullery decided to throw the youngster into the first division melting pot to replace the injured Mark Lawrenson against, ironically, Ipswich Town. The 17-year-old didn't disappoint and was a mainstay for the next three seasons, winning 'Player of the Season' in 1983 and scoring in the never-to-be-forgotten FA Cup Final.

SATURDAY 30th MARCH 1968

Only 5,813 were at the Goldstone to see Kit Napier's strike in the 1-0 Division Three win over Southport. The poor crowd is blamed on the BBC's live coverage of the Grand National.

WEDNESDAY 30th MARCH 1983

Having scored nine league goals for the bottom team in the first division, Michael Robinson was called up by the Republic of Ireland for the last time as an Albion player and played in the 1-0 European Championship qualifying win in Malta.

SATURDAY 31st MARCH 1934

Oliver 'Buster' Brown made his debut in a 3-0 third division (south) win at Gillingham. He went on to score 45 goals in just 66 games.

SATURDAY 31st MARCH 1956

This top-of-the-table showdown at Orient was the second Albion game in as many days. The majority of the 25,550 fans crammed into Brisbane Road go home disappointed. A single second-half goal from Malcolm Stephens secured a priceless victory for Billy Lane's side, who are two points behind the O's but have played two games more.

FRIDAY 31st MARCH 1972

A Torquay United defender admitted a handball to the referee that allowed Albion back into this third division Goldstone fixture. Just under 28,000 fans witnessed a 3-1 victory.

Brighton & Hove Albion

ON THIS DAY

APRIL

FRIDAY 1st APRIL 1949

Future Northern Ireland international Sammy Nelson was born in Belfast. The left-back joined the Albion in September 1981, playing 45 times and scoring once.

SUNDAY 1st APRIL 1973

Albion's Board of Directors decided not to increase admission prices for the three remaining home fixtures of the season in light of tax changes. The club had to pay a value added tax bill which, according to club secretary Ken Calver was around £13,000.

WEDNESDAY 1st APRIL 1987

Midfielder Danny Wilson came on as sub for Northern Ireland in the European Championship 2-0 qualifying defeat to England in Belfast.

SATURDAY 1st APRIL 1989

Albion won 2-1 against Manchester City at the Goldstone. The Maine Road outfit were incensed as chief 'ball-boy' Keith Cuss appeared to head a ball further out of play as the promotion-challenging visitors chased an equaliser. The home side held on for a vital three points in the battle against relegation.

TUESDAY 1st APRIL 1997

Barnet were the visitors for the last-ever floodlit game at the Goldstone Ground. Ian Baird chested in the only goal in front of the North Stand to win the game for the bottom-placed Seagulls. Steve Gritt's rejuvenated side were left just two points behind both Hartlepool United and Hereford United with five games to play.

MONDAY 1st APRIL 2002

Visitors Bristol City conceded the first goal – a glancing Junior Lewis header from a Paul Watson free-kick – but equalised through Tommy Doherty. The end-to-end contest was nearly over – Albion needed three points to go top of Division Two, while the Robins were chasing a play-off spot – when Gary Hart floated over a measured ball. Substitute Lee Steele flung himself goalwards and connected making it 2-1 to the Seagulls. The final whistle blew and Albion were the league leaders.

TUESDAY 2nd APRIL 1963

Gary Howlett was born in Dublin. The Irishman only represented the Albion 37 times, scoring twice, but did play a vital part in the 1983 FA Cup Final – perfectly crossing for Gordon Smith to nod Albion ahead.

SATURDAY 2nd APRIL 1983

Albion enjoyed their fifth successive win on this date. Despite beating Tottenham Hotspur 2-1 in front of 20,359 fans at the Goldstone, the Seagulls were still bottom of the first division.

TUESDAY 2nd APRIL 1985

Trevor Aylott fired past Graham Moseley to give Crystal Palace a 1-0 lead at Selhurst Palace. Then tragedy struck. Opposing defender Henry Hughton scythed down Republic of Ireland striker Gerry Ryan in a shocking challenge. The Irishman's leg was broken, ending his playing career. Spurred on by their team-mate's injury, the Albion fought back and Danny Wilson equalised 10 minutes later.

SATURDAY 3rd APRIL 1965

Archie Macaulay's side moved into second in the fourth division thanks to goals from Jack Smith and Wally Gould in a 2-1 win at Wrexham.

WEDNESDAY 3rd APRIL 1974

A gate of 9,851 saw Barry Bridges, Ronnie Welch, Billy McEwan and Ronnie Howell hit the target in the third division 4-1 thrashing of Cambridge United. It was the best home win under Brian Clough.

SATURDAY 3rd APRIL 1976

Paul Emblen was born in Bromley, Kent. The striker had a fairly innocuous Albion 16-game loan spell but, on Boxing Day 1998, the Charlton player fired in a hat-trick in the 4-4 draw with Colchester United. His other goal came against Cambridge United.

SATURDAY 3rd APRIL 1982

Three coach-loads of supporters from France arrived at the Goldstone to witness a first division fixture with Southampton. Neil McNab scored a first-half penalty in the 1-1 draw before 20,977 fans. However, it was another point dropped in the quest for a UEFA Cup place.

SATURDAY 4th APRIL 1908

A 2-0 Southern League win over Millwall was the first under Jack Robson's stewardship. Frank Scott-Walford's departure to Leeds City had opened the manager's door for the former goalkeeper, who would build the Albion's first successful team by signing players such as Charlie Webb, Billy Booth and Bullet Jones. The Southern League title, Southern Charity Cup and Charity Shield successes alerted Manchester United, who acquired his services in 1914.

MONDAY 4th APRIL 1910

Albion lifted their first trophy of a momentous season with a 1-0 win over Brentford. The Southern Professional Charity Cup Final was played at Stamford Bridge and it took extra-time to separate the two sides. Bullet Jones scored the decisive goal before 3,000 spectators, who saw skipper Joe Leeming presented with the trophy.

THURSDAY 4th APRIL 1929

The small town of Helston, in Cornwall, was the setting for the birth of Mike Tiddy. The outside-right was signed by Billy Lane from Arsenal in 1958 as a 29-year-old and would go on to score 12 goals in 146 Albion games.

SATURDAY 5th APRIL 1952

One of the most experienced men ever to represent the Albion was born in Liverpool. Dennis Mortimer played over 200 times for Coventry before attracting the attention of Aston Villa. Success followed with a 3-2 League Cup win over Everton in 1977, the league title in 1981 and the European Cup win against Bayern Munich in 1982 – where the midfielder wore the captain's armband. Dennis joined the Seagulls in August 1985 and was a virtual ever-present the following campaign – but he only spent one season with the Seagulls and left for Birmingham City a year later.

SATURDAY 5th APRIL 1980

Old foes Albion and Crystal Palace met for the first time in the top flight at Selhurst Park. Peter Ward gave Albion the lead in front of a 31,466 partisan crowd but the home side equalised after the break to send both sides home with a point apiece.

MONDAY 6th APRIL 1953

Tommy Bisset made his debut as a centre-forward in the 3-0 third division (south) defeat at Walsall, but would convert to right-back after playing his first seven Albion games up front.

SATURDAY 6th APRIL 1974

Former England international Barry Bridges was sent off in the 2-1 win over at Walsall at the Goldstone. Brian Powney played in goal with a broken finger as manager Brian Clough had no other fit custodian.

FRIDAY 6th APRIL 1990

Sergei Gotsmanov scored a wonderful goal in the 2-0 home win over Hull City. "Skipping round tackles and holding your arms aloft *before* slotting the ball into the net is the stuff of which dreams are made," raved manager Barry Lloyd.

TUESDAY 6th APRIL 1999

Albion's ninth defeat in 10 games – the other was a draw – resulted in the sack for manager Jeff Wood. Gary Hart scored the Seagulls' consolation in the 3-1 Priestfield defeat to Cambridge United.

SATURDAY 6th APRIL 2002

Albion were on the verge of the first division after a 1-0 win at Peterborough United. Leading scorer Bobby Zamora volleyed home in front of around 4,000 Albion fans in the Moyes End. Gary Hart's leg-break after eight minutes put a dampener on the celebrations.

SATURDAY 7th APRIL 1984

Jonathan Pearce, the new sports producer on Southern Sound, wrote his first column for the programme against Grimsby Town.

WEDNESDAY 7th APRIL 1993

Kurt Nogan started a goalscoring run of seven in five consecutive games with a strike in the 3-1 home win over Mansfield Town.

SUNDAY 7th APRIL 2002

Reading's 2-2 draw at Tranmere Rovers handed Albion a second successive promotion… without kicking a ball!

FRIDAY 8th APRIL 1955

Peter Harburn enjoyed his Albion debut in the 1-1 draw at Priestfield. The big, powerful centre-forward joined the Brentford ground staff in 1946 but joined the Royal Navy as a Boy Seaman a year later. In 1949/50, he represented Uxbridge in the Corinthian League and the following year played for both Portsmouth and Albion's reserve teams, before finally joining the stripes full-time in 1955.

SATURDAY 8th APRIL 1978

With Albion needing the two points for their chase, Alan Mullery took a gamble at Ewood Park with a 4-2-4 formation. Both sides were in the promotion hunt but a defeat would almost certainly mean second division football the following season. Eric Potts scored the only goal five minutes from time.

TUESDAY 8th APRIL 1980

Two goals from Peter Ward and an own-goal secured a 3-0 win over Wolverhampton Wanderers at the Goldstone Ground. It was the first league meeting between the clubs in Sussex and secured a double for Alan Mullery's side, the first of four consecutive doubles over Wolves.

SUNDAY 9th APRIL 1876

Alf Sharp, the first professional footballer signed by a Brighton club, was born in the town. The inside-forward played for Brighton United before joining the Albion in 1901, making just the one appearance against Shepherd's Bush.

TUESDAY 9th APRIL 1912

Lionel Piggin, a left-back on trial from Peterborough City, made his solitary Albion appearance in the 4-1 home Southern League Division One win over Crystal Palace in front of just 2,500 fans. The day before, a Goldstone gate of 10,000 watched as Luton Town were beaten 1-0.

FRIDAY 9th APRIL 1971

A Good Friday crowd of 22,687 – nearly 13,000 more than the season's average – crammed into the Goldstone for the visit of Aston Villa. It was the famous club's first-ever campaign in the third tier but the Midlands side had no answer to Kit Napier's second-half strike.

MONDAY 10th APRIL 1961

The Goldstone Ground switched on its distinctive 'drenchlighting' floodlights – which cost £13,523 – for the first time in a friendly against nine-times champions of Denmark, Boldklubben Frem.

SATURDAY 10th APRIL 1965

Ex-England striker Bobby Smith and defender Norman Gall grabbed the goals in the 2-1 Goldstone victory over Tranmere Rovers. The 24,017 in attendance was the third highest crowd in the country after first division Everton and Newcastle United. This feat is put into perspective when you realise Albion's game was in the fourth division!

SATURDAY 10th APRIL 1982

Terry Neill's Arsenal were the visitors in front of 21,019 fans at the Goldstone Ground. Andy Ritchie and Michael Robinson both struck in the second half to send the Albion up to 10th in the first division with a 2-1 victory.

WEDNESDAY 10th APRIL 1991

Despite being outplayed by West Ham United for much of the game, Albion carved out a 1-0 victory after John Byrne's shot bobbled past goalkeeper Ludek Miklosko and into the North Stand goal.

TUESDAY 11th APRIL 1904

After a meeting at the Royal Pavilion, Brighton & Hove Albion Football Club became a limited company. George Broadbridge, the club's first chairman, is joined on the board by directors Reg Alderton, Charles Bunker, Tom Cooter, Frederick Stevens, Albert Grinyer (licensee of the Albion Inn) and Ben Parker.

SATURDAY 11th APRIL 1953

Steve Burtenshaw made his debut in the 5-1 victory at Exeter City. The wing-half came from a famous local footballing family and joined the Albion ground staff after leaving Portslade Secondary School in 1951. Granted a testimonial in 1963, after 16 years' service, Steve held a variety of coaching roles including posts at Arsenal, QPR and Sheffield Wednesday.

MONDAY 12th APRIL 1971

It was a very happy Easter for the Albion. A 3-2 third division win over Bradford City at Valley Parade was the club's third over the long weekend; the only side in England who managed to earn six out of six points. Pat Saward was rewarded with the first 'Manager of the Month' award for an Albion boss.

TUESDAY 12th APRIL 1977

Albion have only won four times in the 22 fixtures on this date since 1920. On this occasion a brace from Peter Ward – his 32nd and 33rd goals of the season – kept Albion on top of the third division after a 2-0 home win over relegation-threatened Reading.

SATURDAY 12th APRIL 1986

Chairman Brian Bedson wrote an open letter to Albion fans regarding information reported in *The Evening Argus* suggesting that the club do not want promotion to the first division. "The club amassed a deficit of over £1.3m on the trading of players during the 10-year period prior to me joining the board (1983)… All too often this club has been bailed out by selling its assets in the past. The sale of Lawrenson, Robinson and Stevens were all examples." In the same programme, manager Chris Cattlin reveals how Colin Clarke had been recommended: "He had been given two free transfers and suffered a broken leg in the recent past. I spoke to 10 fourth division managers and their assessment was mixed, so I declined to sign him." Clarke went on to score over 100 league goals for Bournemouth, Portsmouth, Southampton and Queens Park Rangers – the latter two in the top flight – and become Northern Ireland's second-highest scorer.

MONDAY 12th APRIL 1999

Albion launched the campaign for a "Yes Yes" vote in the referendum over Falmer. Wearing a green "Yes Yes" T-shirt, new manager Micky Adams walked onto the stage at Hove Town Hall to a standing ovation.

MONDAY 12th APRIL 2004

Paul Reid made his Albion debut in the 0-0 draw with Rushden & Diamonds at Withdean Stadium. The cultured Australian midfielder – who has a degree in Radiography – arrived from Bradford City.

MONDAY 13th APRIL 1914

Joe Leeming was granted a benefit game and stepped down from the first team in order to play in the reserves against Southampton on Easter Monday when a good turnout could be expected. Around 3,500 supporters attended the 3-2 win at the Goldstone, netting the full-back £118.

FRIDAY 13th APRIL 1979

Albion enjoyed their second-highest gate of the campaign, as a crowd of 30,859 packed the Goldstone for the second division visit of Charlton Athletic. After just 11 minutes, following a partially-cleared free-kick, midfielder Paul Clark smashed the ball home from 25 yards. An own-goal, midway through the second half, made it 2-0 to Albion and secured maximum points. The win put them top of the division, two points from Sunderland with Crystal Palace and Stoke City a further point away, and was the first-ever victory on this date since the club became a league side.

TUESDAY 13th APRIL 1999

Just 2,207 hardy souls were present at Priestfield for Micky Adams' first 'home' game in charge – a 1-0 win over Shrewsbury Town.

SATURDAY 13th APRIL 2002

The penultimate fixture of the season and the final match at Withdean – the 2002 World Cup was the reason behind the earlier-than-usual conclusion to the domestic football season. It was a home match with Swindon Town and there's plenty at stake. A fairly forgettable 90 minutes of football will be consigned to a small section of the history books – but Albion fans who were there didn't really care too much about that. What will be remembered were the events after the final whistle. Brentford drew at Queens Park Rangers, and Reading shared four goals at Peterborough United, which meant Albion won the second division title. Club captain Paul Rogers lifted the championship trophy for a second successive season. On this date 15 league fixtures have been played since 1920, with a noticeable paucity of goals. Eight draws include five stalemates, and just one game when the Albion registered more than one strike; the 2-0 win over Charlton in 1979.

SATURDAY 14th APRIL 1951

Ray Garbutt, Jess Willard, Johnny McNichol and Glen Wilson got the goals as Albion record a comprehensive 4-0 third division (south) Goldstone victory over Ipswich Town.

SATURDAY 14th APRIL 2001

A healthy contingent from Sussex was present at Home Park to see Albion take on Plymouth Argyle. Three points would be enough for an automatic promotion spot from the third division, as long as Hartlepool lose and Rochdale fail to win, despite the fact there are six games remaining. Paul Brooker netted from a corner after three minutes and Bobby Zamora struck 13 minutes later to send the visitors in 2-0 up at half-time. Rochdale drew at Macclesfield Town while Hull City take the lead at Victoria Park – and keep it until the final whistle. Albion are up!

WEDNESDAY 15th APRIL 1970

An inconsistent run meant promotion could be achieved if Orient lost their five games in hand and Albion walloped Mansfield Town at the Goldstone Ground. A 2-1 defeat leaves the Seagulls on 55 points in fifth – the east London club go up as eventual third division champions.

SATURDAY 15th APRIL 1978

Tottenham Hotspur made their first league visit to the Goldstone Ground. It's the London club's only season away from the top flight in 57 years and 32,647 fans see a 3-1 win secured with goals from Paul Clark, Graham Winstanley and Eric Potts. As a consequence of the violence caused by Spurs fans, a perimeter fence was erected the following season.

FRIDAY 15th APRIL 1988

In an interview in the match programme, Albion midfielder Adrian Owers saw into the future by predicting the end of the back-pass to the goalkeeper. It became law four years later.

SATURDAY 15th APRIL 1992

Derby fan Edward Wood was a guest of the club directors as the Goldstone is the 94th ground he's visited in 243 days.

WEDNESDAY 16th APRIL 1969

Centre-half John Napier won the club's inaugural Player of the Season award. Alex Dawson and John Templeman were runners-up.

MONDAY 16th APRIL 1990

Not quite as successful as his brother Marco, Ricardo Gabbiadini played for just 14 minutes in an Albion shirt. The forward came on for Kevin Bremner in the 3-0 second division defeat at Portsmouth.

SATURDAY 16th APRIL 1983

Hundreds on coaches departed the Greyhound Stadium and snaked their way to north London; it was FA Cup semi-final day! Albion had avoided Manchester United and Arsenal and were drawn against Sheffield Wednesday at Highbury. Jimmy Case continued his goalscoring run by smashing a 35-yard free-kick against the underside of the bar, and in, to give the Albion a 14th-minute lead. Yugoslav international midfielder Ante Mirocevic scrambled home an equaliser before Michael Robinson swivelled and shot to fire the Seagulls to Wembley for the first time in their 82-year history!

WEDNESDAY 16th APRIL 1986

It was popular manager Chris Cattlin's last game as Albion manager. The North Stand held up banners pleading for the former left-back to stay but the Rock Shop boss is off. He said that he "managed the club because he wanted to, not because he needed to".

TUESDAY 16th APRIL 1991

A bit of history was made at Portsmouth's Fratton Park. The first Romanian to play in the Football League, Stefan Iovan, made his Albion debut. The defender played in two European Cup Finals with Steaua Bucharest – beating Barcelona on penalties in 1986 and losing 4-0 to AC Milan in 1989 – and also won 34 caps for his country. Arguably the most experienced player to ever don the stripes.

SATURDAY 16th APRIL 1994

"Johnny Crumplin, football genius!" reverberated around the Racecourse Ground in Wrexham. The right-back scored direct from a corner – falling over as he struck the ball – in the 3-1 win.

SATURDAY 17th APRIL 1982

The end of season slump started here… A Michael Robinson effort at Notts County didn't make a dent in the Magpies' tally of four. Just a couple of months earlier, Mike Bailey' side had been in contention for a UEFA Cup place. Six defeats in the last seven games ended the European dream.

SATURDAY 17th APRIL 2004

Leon Knight slotted his 26th goal of the season as Albion recorded their eighth home win in nine: 1-0 over Peterborough United.

MONDAY 17th APRIL 2006

It was the third-to-last game of the season and Sheffield Wednesday were the visitors to Withdean Stadium. Albion had to win to have any chance of remaining in the Championship; the Owls were one place, and seven points, above. Gary Hart turned the ball into his own net after just eight minutes and Burton O'Brien rounded Wayne Henderson to fire into an empty net with 20 minutes left. Dean Hammond was sent off towards the final whistle to end two battling years just one division away from the Premiership.

WEDNESDAY 18th APRIL 1951

Albion historians were reaching for their record books as the team smashes the best-ever victory in the Football League (equalled in 1965) with a 9-1 annihilation of Newport County at the Goldstone. Both clubs were lying in mid-table as the home side went into the break two up. Then the floodgates opened: Johnny McNichol scored four, while Ken Bennett (2) and Doug Keene also featured on the scoresheet. Des Tennant and Jack Mansell both scored penalties.

TUESDAY 18th APRIL 1978

A great start for Graham Moseley on his goalkeeping debut for the Albion: a clean sheet in the 4-0 win at Bristol Rovers.

SATURDAY 18th APRIL 1981

Albion completed a league double over Crystal Palace at Selhurst Park. John Gregory (2) and Gordon Smith netted the goals in the resounding 3-0 victory.

WEDNESDAY 19th APRIL 1972

It was the first-ever league meeting between the Albion and Blackburn Rovers at the Goldstone Ground. Goals from Willie Irvine, Ken Beamish and Brian Bromley – in front of 23,269 – kept Pat Saward's men in the promotion picture with a 3-0 home win. Albion stayed second behind leaders Aston Villa.

SATURDAY 19th APRIL 1980

The penultimate home game of the season resulted in a 2-1 win over Middlesbrough, but events off the pitch grabbed the headlines. A few hours after the last of the 20,427 fans had made their way home, the South Stand was in flames. The wooden seating and supporting structure was destroyed, leaving just the roof. The stand re-opened as an all-seater the following season.

SATURDAY 19th APRIL 2003

Leicester City need three points from a first division fixture at the Walkers Bowl. Old friend of the Albion Micky Adams was in charge of the home side, who duly get the required result to leapfrog Pompey at the top and earn a place in the Premiership. At the final whistle, the former Seagulls boss is straight over to the away end to applaud the 3,000-plus travelling army from Sussex.

SATURDAY 20th APRIL 1985

Irishman Adrian Walsh – keepie-uppie world record holder with a total of 12,104 – demonstrated his juggling skills before the Goldstone's 17,279 fans who witness the 1-1 draw with Leeds United.

MONDAY 20th APRIL 1987

A 14-game run without a win came to the end at the Goldstone Ground – against old adversaries Crystal Palace. Danny Wilson and Darren Hughes were the heroes as the Albion beat Palace 2-0. Unfortunately, the victory still leaves Albion six points adrift at the foot of Division Two.

SATURDAY 20th APRIL 1991

Albion are humbled 3-0 at the Goldstone by Oxford United. Although it probably didn't soften the blow, the U's boss was Brian Horton and his captain was… Steve Foster.

WEDNESDAY 21st APRIL 1926

Ernie Ison made his debut against Southend United. The outside-left is the holder of an Albion record that is unlikely ever to be surpassed; the former collier made over 300 appearances for the reserves! The consistent form of Tug Wilson kept out the loyal Midlander, who played just 16 times for the first XI.

SATURDAY 21st APRIL 1979

Albion draw 1-1 in Bedfordshire. In the Luton programme, future Albion full-back Sammy Nelson was mentioned after the Northern Irishman bared his buttocks at the Coventry City fans at Highfield Road after baiting from the terraces. On the same day, Hove liberal candidate Dr James Walsh suggested closing Shoreham Airport to build a new home for Albion: "I think it's vital the club moves from its present restricting facilities at the Goldstone. Several alternatives have been mentioned, including Withdean Stadium and Corals. One large area cries out for development and that's Shoreham Airport. In short, it could become the regional sports and leisure centre of the south, on a par with Crystal Palace."

THURSDAY 22nd APRIL 1954

Albion were weighing up pre-season tour options: Germany, Belgium or the south of France? On the same day it was announced that two former Albion full-backs, Stan Willemse and Jack Mansell, had been picked by the FA for two continental tours in May.

SATURDAY 22nd APRIL 1989

A week after the tragic events at Hillsborough, Albion played Swindon Town at the Goldstone. The game kicked off at 3.06 pm – which was when the FA Cup semi-final had been abandoned. The minute's silence was impeccably observed and £5,665 was collected for the appeal fund.

SATURDAY 22nd APRIL 1957

Jeff Darey made the first of his 11 appearances in an Albion shirt, after four seasons on the books at the Goldstone Ground! The striker arrived from Chelsea as a part-time professional but struggled to make an impression as Peter Harburn and Adrian Thorne continued to bang in the goals.

SATURDAY 23rd APRIL 1910

After sitting top of the league since early February, Albion won their first-ever championship by beating Swindon Town, their closest rivals, in front of 11,000 spectators at the Goldstone. Bullet Jones netted twice, with local boy Bert Longstaff grabbing the other, meaning Brighton lifted the trophy with a game to spare. *The Argus* reported; 'Every preparation was made for the accommodation of a big crowd… Extra seating was provided on the west side, and it was needed… All the ring seats and the open stand rapidly became packed, and still the turnstiles clicked in a way that suggested a harvest of silver for the Albion's exchequer'.

MONDAY 23rd APRIL 1962

Albion are relegated with a game to spare, going down 3-0 to Norwich City at Carrow Road. The Seagulls drew at home, and lost away, to eventual second division champions Liverpool.

MONDAY 23rd APRIL 1979

John Vinicombe reported in *The Argus*: 'The new Brighton bypass will play a vital part in deciding the site of the proposed £7m home for Brighton & Hove Albion… It must be no fewer than 55 acres with space for 7,000 cars. The stadium would contain 25,000 seats and room for 10,000 standing. The purpose would be to attract all the family and to include facilities for other sports. The site could be possibly shared by a giant supermarket'.

SATURDAY 23rd APRIL 1983

Terry Connor scored in the 1-0 home victory over Dave Sexton's Coventry City. The win gave the club a sniff of first division survival. The programme carried a full-page advert on how fans can get their FA Cup Final tickets.

TUESDAY 23rd APRIL 1996

A must-win match for both Notts County, who were pushing for promotion, and Albion, who were fighting for survival. Just 3,501 fans are present at Meadow Lane to witness the 2-1 defeat; the reverse condemns Albion to relegation into the Football League's basement for the first time since 1965.

SATURDAY 24th APRIL 1909

Albion needed just one point from their Goldstone date with Norwich City to avoid relegation from Southern League Division One. Scottish inside-forward Jimmy Robertson calmed the nerves of the 5,000 present by netting Albion's only goal in a 1-1 draw.

TUESDAY 24th APRIL 1973

Without tasting victory on the road since a 2-0 victory at Huddersfield Town on October 14th, it's no surprise that Albion were relegated from Division Two after a 2-0 defeat at QPR's Loftus Road.

SATURDAY 24th APRIL 1982

Ray Wilkins scored the only goal for Manchester United in their 1-0 victory over the Albion in Hove. Norman Whiteside debuts for United.

THURSDAY 25th APRIL 1910

The Mayor's Parlour in Hove Town Hall was the venue for the Brighton & Hove Albion dinner. The morning dress occasion was believed to be the first football dinner in the towns for over 25 years. The cost was five shillings and, with each ticket, a lady could be admitted to the balconies at 8.30pm.

SATURDAY 25th APRIL 1959

The last game of the season was the first game of a remarkable run. Jack Bertolini would go on to enjoy a run of 193 consecutive matches. The right-half, born of Italian ancestry in Scotland, joined Albion in 1958 instead of Huddersfield Town after his wife took a liking to the south coast. He made a total of 279 starts and scored 14 goals.

SATURDAY 25th APRIL 1981

Going into the game Albion were only out of the first division drop-zone courtesy of a better goal difference than relegation rivals Coventry City. The team knew that a win at Sunderland's Roker Park was vital as the Seagulls aimed for a third successive season in the top flight. Michael Robinson scored his 22nd goal of the campaign in the first half only for Alan Brown to equalise. With the clock ticking down, Gordon Smith crossed for left-back Gary Williams to smash home a last-minute winner.

MONDAY 26th APRIL 1965

Unbeaten at home all season, Albion hosted Darlington needing just a point for promotion from the fourth division. The omens were in the home side's favour: five straight Goldstone victories, 15 goals scored and just three conceded. The forward line was led by former England international Bobby Smith – he scored once – and was ably assisted by namesake Jack – who got one too – and winger Wally Gould who grabbed another. The final score of 3-1, in front of a huge Hove crowd of 31,423, saw the Albion clinch the championship with 63 points (two for a win) after scoring 102 goals through the course of the league season.

SATURDAY 26th APRIL 1997

The curtain comes down on 95 years of football at the Goldstone Ground. The famous old stadium – loved by thousands across the globe – hosted its final match, after being sold to property developers. Doncaster Rovers were the opponents in conditions rather apt for the occasion; grey, overcast and rainy. A two-minute Last Post is played by a lone trumpeter before the teams emerged. In the Director's Box for the first time was chairman-elect Dick Knight, with his colleagues Bob Pinnock and Martin Perry. A scrappy, nervy affair was brought to life in the 16th minute when Albion forward Ian Baird and Rovers defender Darren Moore were sent off for fighting. In the 68th minute winger Stuart Storer side-footed a volley into the roof of the net after Mark Morris had headed against the Doncaster Rovers bar. The souvenir hunters invaded the pitch on the final whistle after the Albion had got the precious three points they required. One vital game left for the season: Hereford away... where Albion must at least draw to survive in the Football League.

SATURDAY 26th APRIL 2003

Watford visited Withdean Stadium for a Championship encounter. The Hornets had beaten Burnley 7-4 at Turf Moor just three weeks prior to this game. Albion needed three points to have any chance of avoiding relegation and got off to a flyer when Dean Blackwell headed home after 13 minutes. Paul Kitson, Bobby Zamora and Charlie Oatway completed the scoring in a convincing 4-0 victory. Meanwhile fans also cheered on arch rivals Crystal Palace, as they kept Albion in with a slim chance of avoiding relegation by beating relegation rivals Stoke City 1-0.

MONDAY 27th APRIL 1903

The club's first play-off game was a 'test match' against Watford at the Canning Town Memorial Ground, home of West Ham United. A place in the Southern League's first division was up for grabs. Albion had finished joint champions of Division Two while Watford were at the foot of Division One. Only 200 spectators saw a 5-3 victory. A larger crowd greeted the team back at Brighton Station and escorted them to the club's headquarters, the Seven Stars in Ship Street.

SATURDAY 27th APRIL 1957

It was 3-3 at half-time in a third division (south) fixture – but a second-half deluge from the Albion attack shocked Reading. Roy Jennings, Dennis Foreman (2), Jeff Darey, Frankie Howard and Albert Mundy, with a hat-trick, are all on target in the 8-3 hammering.

TUESDAY 27th APRIL 1982

Mickey Thomas made his third of five Wales international appearances while at the Goldstone – but England win 1-0 in Cardiff.

SATURDAY 27th APRIL 1996

The natives were getting restless at the Goldstone, and with very good reason. A 'no profit' clause was removed from the club's constitution, meaning the club's home for over 90 years could be sold to Chartwell and the directors could have closed the club down and taken the profits. No announcement had been made as to where Albion would play their home games the following campaign and added to that the club had just suffered relegation to the basement for the first time since 1965. Understandably the atmosphere among the 9,852 in attendance for the final home game of the season with York City was one of sheer fury. The game lasted just 16 minutes. With the score at 0-0 thousands of loyal Albion fans invaded the pitch and snapped both crossbars forcing the referee to abandon the fixture. Exacerbated by their club's plight, supporters from across the county had organised the protest in order to gain national media attention – it worked – but it didn't save the Goldstone Ground. Two days later, the club announced a deal with new owners Chartwell to lease back the stadium for one last season. The cost had been quoted as £400,000 by Chartwell, a figure Albion chief executive David Bellotti refused to confirm or deny.

SATURDAY 28TH APRIL 1934

For the second time in three days Albion lost 4-3. Charlton Athletic are 4-1 up at the break before Buster Brown scored two – taking his tally to nine in four games – in the second period.

WEDNESDAY 28th APRIL 1954

Albion need to win at Crystal Palace for any chance of promotion to Division Two for the first time. Amateur forward Morton converted a cross from ex-Albion winger Wally Hanlon to put the Selhurst side in the lead (55), before Jimmy Leadbitter equalised on the hour. Jack Arlidge's Postbag column in that day's *Evening Argus* was full of debate over Albion's recent dip in form that had cost the club any chance of promotion. A mixture of bitter disappointment and admiration for their spirited fight is characterised by Nobby Clarke of Freshfield Road, Brighton: "…what does it matter which division we are in? I say again, well done and good luck for next season. To blazes with the 'Dismal Jimmies'."

SATURDAY 28th APRIL 1962

Young Sussex-born goalkeeper Brian Powney made his Albion debut in the last game of the season at Derby County. The Seaford custodian holds the record number of appearances for the man between the sticks – 386 – and shared testimonials with fellow long-serving stalwart Norman Gall, in 1971 and 1972. Away from football, a certain Chris Ramsey, right-back for Albion in the 1983 FA Cup Final, was born in Birmingham.

SATURDAY 28th APRIL 1979

The smoke-bomb thrown from the South Stand caused confusion as Teddy Maybank opened the scoring against Blackburn Rovers. The goal was allowed and another from Andy Rollings sealed the 2-1 second division win in front of 26,141 fans.

TUESDAY 28th APRIL 1981

Jacob Cohen made his fourth appearance for Israel during his time at the Albion, in a 3-1 defeat to Scotland in Glasgow. Signed from Maccabi Tel Aviv, the left-back made just six appearances for the first team during his brief sojourn on the south coast.

SATURDAY 29th APRIL 1978

Albion entertained Blackpool in this vital end-of-season encounter. The Seagulls needed to beat their fellow seasiders – and hope Southampton triumphed over Tottenham Hotspur at The Dell (both of whom were in the hunt to go up) – if they were going to win promotion to the top flight for the first time in the club's history. Peter Ward and Brian Horton scored to earn a 2-1 win but a goalless draw at the Dell meant Saints and Spurs went up instead. Post-match, Alan Mullery addresses the despondent fans from the West Stand and confidently (and correctly) predicted that supporters wouldn't have to wait too long for the big step up.

SATURDAY 29th APRIL 1995

Former Everton and Bolton winger Stuart Storer netted on his Albion debut at Birmingham City. The crowd favourite – signed from Exeter City for £15,000 by Liam Brady – scored 15 times in 150 Seagulls appearances and famously netted the last-ever goal at the Goldstone Ground against Doncaster Rovers.

SATURDAY 30th APRIL 1907

Jack Hall became the first Albion player to exceed 30 goals in a season with his brace in the 3-3 United League draw with Crystal Palace. The centre-forward was also the first player to hit the net more than 50 times for the club.

SATURDAY 30th APRIL 1958

After spending their entire Football League existence in the third division (south), Albion stood on the threshold of promotion to the second tier for the first time. Sitting in third place with a game remaining, the top two sides – Plymouth Argyle and Brentford, who were in pole position on goal difference – had no games left. An Albion defeat would send the Bees up – but Hove-born Adrian Thorne fired in five against Watford in front of 31,038 Goldstone fans to clinch the home side's first Football League title in a 6-0 win.

SATURDAY 30th APRIL 1988

The matchday programme finished runner-up in the third division awards and 17th overall in the Football League.

Brighton & Hove Albion

ON THIS DAY

MAY

SATURDAY 1st MAY 1948

Swansea Town's Vetch Field was the venue for the last game of the season. Albion needed a win to avoid re-election to the third division (south). Sadly, it was not to be as the two teams played out a goalless draw. Just five points separated the bottom ten sides.

TUESDAY 1st MAY 2001

Withdean Stadium was full of fans waving brown envelopes in reference to Chesterfield's off-the-field problems and rogue chairman Darren Brown's wrongdoings. The majority of the 6,847 in attendance were hoping to see the Albion win and therefore lift their first championship trophy in 36 years. In an emotional and historical evening at the club's temporary home, it was fitting that dependable defender Danny Cullip should rise to thump home a header to win Albion the title. The players were presented with the trophy and individual medals at the final whistle.

SATURDAY 1st MAY 2004

Albion hosted Notts County at Withdean. An own-goal from County's 18-year-old debutant defender Kelvin Wilson gave Albion the win, and earns three points which ensured the club's place in the end-of-season play-offs.

FRIDAY 2nd MAY 1958

second division clubs were happy to welcome newly-promoted Albion. Bristol Rovers manager Bert Tann said: "Brighton will be attractive opposition for us, and we look forward to renewing our rivalry with them on the field." Cardiff City assistant manager Bill Jones commented: "We know and like Brighton in this part of the world." Allan Brown, Sunderland boss said: "There'll be a big welcome here for them, take it from me."

SATURDAY 2nd MAY 1992

With the second division championship secured, Ipswich Town fans flocked to Portman Road. It was slightly different for the 2,000-plus Albion fans in attendance; a victory – and other teams' results going in their favour – was the Seagulls only hope. Despite a Raphael Meade strike, a 3-1 defeat meant third division football the following season.

SATURDAY 2nd MAY 1981

The great escape is completed! Albion had won their last three games to give them a chance of staying the first division, and went into the match against Leeds United at the Goldstone knowing victory would guarantee top-flight football for a third season. On the half-hour mark, the ball fell to Steve Foster who dashed through to give his side the lead. Record signing Andy Ritchie made it two with 10 minutes remaining and the Albion were safe!

SATURDAY 3rd MAY 1958

Just weeks after the Munich air disaster, Manchester United lost to two Nat Lofthouse goals in the FA Cup Final against Bolton Wanderers. Wearing red that day were Freddie Goodwin and Alex Dawson. The former signed the latter for Albion 10 years later.

WEDNESDAY 3rd MAY 1972

Just four days earlier Rochdale's Spotland was the venue for a 2-1 Albion victory. A bumper crowd of 34,766 packs the Goldstone for the return fixture to see if the Seagulls can get the point they need for promotion to the second division. John Templeman – who arrived in Hove after the disbandment of the Portsmouth reserve side in 1966 – scored the goal in a 1-1 draw to earn the priceless point required.

TUESDAY 3rd MAY 1977

It was the last home game of the season. Sheffield Wednesday attract 30,756 Goldstone spectators; the 15th 20,000-plus attendance of the season. Albion win 3-2 with strikes from goal machine Peter Ward, a Brian Horton spot-kick and one from Steve Piper, who would go on to be an ever-present for the campaign. Albion achieved promotion to the second division with two games spare, but both end in defeat to hand the title to Mansfield Town.

THURSDAY 3rd MAY 2007

The Seagulls Party – formed to stand in the Lewes District against councillors who oppose the club's new stadium – fared well at local elections: Steve Williams (Lewes Priory) polled 431 votes; Mark Jackson (Newhaven Denton and Meeching) 523; Roz South (Lewes Bridge) 262 and Edward Bassford (Ouse Valley and Ringmer) 467.

SATURDAY 3rd MAY 1997

Quite possibly the most important game in the history of Brighton
& Hove Albion Football Club: Hereford United versus the Albion
at Edgar Street. It was the last game of the season. Both clubs could
drop out of the Football League: the Bulls needed to win and the
Seagulls needed just a point to avoid the dreaded demotion to the
Conference. With no venue for home games secured for the following
season, Albion fans across the world realised this could be the club's
last game – ever. The 3,500 plus away fans felt a sense of foreboding
after 20 minutes when Sussex-born Kerry Mayo turned a Tony Agana
cross past his own goalkeeper, Mark Ormerod. After a dreadfully
sombre half-time the players re-entered the fray to a tumultuous roar
of encouragement from the away end. Steve Gritt played his trump
card in the 55th minute; the injured Paul McDonald is taken off and
replaced by striker Robbie Reinelt. Within eight minutes the £15,000
purchase from Colchester United had made his mark. Craig Maskell
controlled a poor defensive clearance on his knee before smashing a
left-foot volley against the right-hand post from 20 yards. Reinelt –
alert to the opportunity – won a short sprint with two defenders to drill
home in the bottom corner. Cue pandemonium on the terraces! There
were still 30 minutes remaining and the players are almost as nervous
as the fans, some of whom literally couldn't face the action and turned
their backs, such was the tension. In the final few moments, Craig
Maskell went clean through but fired wide. The ball went straight up
the other end and found Adrian Foster bearing down on Ormerod
who kept his nerve as the opposition forward shot straight at him.
Albion were safe! For the players, fans and officials of both clubs the
game is one which will stay in the memory for a very long time.

FRIDAY 4th MAY 1979

The players relaxed with a round of golf at Gosforth Park before the biggest game in the club's 78-year history: at Newcastle United.

SATURDAY 4th MAY 1982

Michael Robinson and Sammy Nelson scored in the penultimate home game of the season – a 2-0 victory over Wolverhampton Wanderers. The programme documented the fact that the club had six players away on international duty the previous week: Steve Foster (England), Mickey Thomas (Wales), Nelson (Northern Ireland), plus Robinson, Tony Grealish and Gerry Ryan with the Republic of Ireland.

SATURDAY 4th MAY 1985

It was reported in the home match programme for the game against Wolverhampton Wanderers, that the team had flown to the previous match at Middlesbrough. Discussing the difference in temperature between north and south, 'Scene Around the Goldstone' mentions the blizzard coming off the North Sea and that hardest hit was Alan Biley: 'He reached the aircraft doorway with his jacket over his arm and sunglasses very prominent'.

MONDAY 4th MAY 1987

With only two away victories in the league all season, Albion travelled to Bradford City for the penultimate game needing all three points for any chance of second division survival. It was not to be; the Bantams triumphed 2-0.

SUNDAY 4th MAY 2003

Blundell Park was the venue for Albion's last-ditch attempt to stay in the first division. Grimsby Town were already relegated and the Seagulls needed to win – and rely on Reading beating Stoke City at the Britannia Stadium – to retain their second-tier status. Michael Keane's spot-kick (23) is equalised from 12 yards by Bobby Zamora on the stroke of half-time. Captain Danny Cullip fired his side into the lead two minutes into the second period and then news filtered through that former Albion loanee Ade Akinbiyi had scored for Stoke. Richard Hughes tapped in past 44-year-old Dave Beasant on the hour to condemn the visitors to the second division next season.

FRIDAY 5th MAY 1972

Defender Norman Gall and goalkeeper Brian Powney – 874 appearances between them – enjoyed a joint testimonial game against Chelsea at the Goldstone Ground in front of 14,230 supporters.

SATURDAY 5th MAY 1979

Over 10,000 Albion fans made the long journey to Newcastle to see if their team can join the elite of English football for the first time. Bizarrely, as Sunderland were also in the hunt for promotion, a healthy contingent of Mackems who couldn't make it to Wrexham were cheering on their bitter rivals at St. James' Park! It didn't make any difference – Brian Horton's diving header from a Gary Williams cross put the visitors ahead. Peter Ward made it two and Gerry Ryan claimed a third before half-time. The first division was just 45 minutes away! Manager Alan Mullery was clearly over-excited as he tore his players off a strip during the interval but they held on – despite the Magpies pulling one back – to claim their well-deserved place among the elite of English football. The manager christened the Seagull Special train the "Paralytic Special" as it snaked its way back to Sussex jam-packed with players, staff and fans celebrating the greatest day in the club's history, so far. On TV that evening was Rolf on Saturday, Dad's Army, The Val Doonican Show, The Rockford Files, Celebrity Squares and Match of the Day.

WEDNESDAY 5th MAY 1999

It was 'Operation Morning Surprise', part of the supporters' campaign for a good turnout in the council's referendum on the new stadium. Brighton & Hove awakes to over four thousand green Yes-Yes balloons tied to lamp-posts across the area to remind the electorate to vote.

SATURDAY 6th MAY 1933

Albion walloped Bristol City 7-0 in the last game of the season at the Goldstone. The gate was 3,645.

THURSDAY 6th MAY 1999

The referendum results showed an 83 per cent vote in favour of the council assisting the Albion to find a permanent home in the Brighton and Hove area, and a 68 per cent vote in favour of Falmer.

SATURDAY 7th MAY 1988

Six straight wins, then a draw at Chester City, in their last seven fixtures moved Albion from sixth to an automatic promotion position in second. The nerves of the vast majority of the 19,800 crowd were eased in the 14th minute when Scottish striker Kevin Bremner stooped to head home against Bristol Rovers. Garry Nelson grabbed his 32nd goal of the campaign almost straight from the second-half kick-off to fire Albion two up. A consolation isn't enough and the Albion are up!

SATURDAY 7th MAY 1983

With minds perhaps focussed on the FA Cup Final, the Albion were relegated by a defeat at home to Manchester City – who gain revenge for the 4-0 FA Cup drubbing back in January – in the penultimate game of the season.

SATURDAY 9th MAY 1925

Ray Garbutt was born in Middlesbrough. The striker – 17 goals in 32 games – survived his vessel sinking during the D-Day landings and joined from Watford in a straight swap for Cyril Thompson in 1951.

WEDNESDAY 8th MAY 1963

A 1-0 defeat at Bournemouth & Boscombe Athletic condemned Albion to their second successive relegation. Champions Northampton Town – on their rise to a solitary season in the top flight – beat Albion 3-0 at the three-sided County Ground, and 5-0 at the Goldstone.

TUESDAY 8th MAY 1979

Chairman Mike Bamber called for a referendum in Brighton and Hove about building a multi-sports complex at Toads Hole Valley.

SUNDAY 8th MAY 2005

Ipswich Town were the visitors to Withdean for this final fixture of the campaign. Albion need just a point to retain their Championship status next season. 'Player of the Season' Adam Virgo missed a clearance after just four minutes to let Finnish striker Shefki Kuqi through to score. However, Brighton-born Virgo made amends a few minutes later by smashing home the rebound from Gary Hart's header on the half-volley and earned the Seagulls the required point.

TUESDAY 9th MAY 1978

Lorenzo Pinamonte was born in Foggia, Italy. After arriving on loan from Bristol City, the tall striker featured in nine Albion games – scoring his only two goals against Exeter City at Withdean in January 1999 – before moving to Brentford.

SATURDAY 9th MAY 1987

Terry Connor (Player of the Year), Darren Hughes, Danny Wilson and Kieran O'Regan make their last Albion appearances as three thousand Leeds United fans run amok after their 1-0 Goldstone victory. On a lighter note in the match programme, Tony Millard recalled a dinner conversation with comedian and Liverpool fan Stan Boardman: 'Stan was a lifeguard at Black Rock and applied for a trial at the Goldstone and was turned down. He was offended as he'd played a couple of times for Liverpool's junior side," said Stan. "I hated Brighton and did so even more when they twice knocked the Reds out of the FA Cup'.'

THURSDAY 9th MAY 1996

Following the abandonment of the original game by a pitch invasion, Albion hosted York City for a morning kick-off. A gate of just 2,106 was watched over by a heavy police presence. The Minstermen won 3-1 and escaped relegation to the third division. John Byrne, Dean Wilkins and Ian Chapman made their last appearances in the stripes, as did Stuart Myall and Junior McDougald.

TUESDAY 10th MAY 1977

Peter Ward scored his 31st league goal to set a new club record in the 2-1 defeat at Swindon Town. The game was rearranged following the abandonment on New Year's Day. Alan Mullery's team needed a win to move ahead of Mansfield Town in the third division championship race.

THURSDAY 10th MAY 1979

The Evening Argus reported that 'champagne could be flowing at thirty thousand feet above America tomorrow as the Seagulls celebrate being second division champions'. Albion were flying to the States for an end-of-season tour as Crystal Palace beat Burnley the following day in front of 51,801 Selhurst Park fans to claim the title.

SATURDAY 11th MAY 1968

Paul Bence's senior career with Albion lasted just 13 minutes. The Littlehampton-born defender came on as substitute in the final game of the season at Walsall, a 2-1 victory.

SATURDAY 11th MAY 1985

With a line-up including the flamboyant Frank Worthington, Albion took on Sheffield United at the Goldstone Ground hoping for three points and for other results to go their way. Unfortunately, despite a 1-0 win over the Blades, Manchester City thrashed Charlton Atheltic 5-1 and the Seagulls finished the season in sixth place, just behind Blackburn Rovers and Portsmouth.

SATURDAY 11th MAY 1991

A run of a solitary victory in six games meant the Seagulls must beat Ipswich Town in Hove to stay in contention of a trip to Wembley. Mike Small fired the home side in front before 'Player of the Year' Perry Digweed saved a penalty from Chris Kiwomya; who would eventually level the scores with ten minutes remaining. In the final minute John Byrne was fouled just outside the box and the seconds ticked down as Dean Wilkins and Robert Codner debated who should take the direct free-kick. The former usurped the latter and curled the ball into the top corner past the despairing dive of goalkeeper Phil Parkes to spark wild scenes on the terraces. Albion were in the play-offs!

WEDNESDAY 12th MAY 1926

Albion's second-highest peacetime scorer of all-time, Albert Mundy, was born is Gosport, Hampshire. The forward topped the goalscoring charts three times after moving along the coast from Portsmouth in 1953. During his five-year spell, Albert netted an impressive 90 times in just 178 starts.

SATURDAY 12th MAY 1984

Albion's only league game on this date was at Newcastle United for Kevin Keegan's last appearance. Although Gerry Ryan scored for the Seagulls they were unable to deflate the 36,415 Geordie hero-worshippers who celebrated a 3-1 win and promotion to the top flight.

THURSDAY 13th MAY 1909

Familiar to dedicated Albion fans, Gillingham was the birthplace of Bert Stephens. The prolific outside-left would surely have become Albion's all-time top scorer if it had not been for the outbreak of World War II. Bert had hit the target 87 times before the hostilities, and would net 174 times in all 366 appearances over a 13-year period.

MONDAY 13th MAY 1974

Brian Clough declared that chairman Mike Bamber could look forward to promotion from the third division next season. Bamber said he would want £1 million for his managerial partnership. As it turned out, Clough left for Leeds two months later and the Seagulls finished 19th. Albion eventually received £45,000 in compensation and Taylor rejoined Clough at Nottingham Forest in 1976.

SATURDAY MAY 14th 1977

Peter Ward scored his last league goal of the season to complete a tally of 32 – and 36 overall in all competitions.

SATURDAY MAY 14th 1983

After scoring 99 times for Pontardawe Athletic over three seasons in the Welsh league Chris Rodon made his Albion debut. Already relegated, the Welshman came on with 15 minutes remaining of the Albion's final first division encounter, a 2-1 defeat at Norwich City. It was his only appearance for Albion as he became homesick and returned to South Wales in August.

FRIDAY 14th MAY 1999

'Bring Home the Albion' campaign spokesman Adrian Newnham handed in a 32,355-signature petition, in 16 binders, to Lord Bassam, leader of Brighton & Hove Council, outside Brighton Town Hall.

TUESDAY 14th MAY 1963

Brixton, South London, was the birthplace of Mark Gall. The striker began his football career at Greenwich Borough before moving to Conference side Maidstone United in 1989 for £2,000. The striker arrived on the coast in October 1991 and immediately made an impact scoring 14 goals in his first season. A knee injury meant he retired at just 29.

FRIDAY 15th MAY 1970

In 1970, Albion played CD Carabanchel as part of Madrid's San Isidro Fiesta, the fourth game of a post-season holiday tour of Spain. A penalty from Alan Duffy, plus goals from Paul Flood and Kit Napier, gave Albion a 3-1 victory.

SATURDAY 15th MAY 1982

A 2-1 defeat against relegated Leeds United at Elland Road was Albion's only league game on this date. The result gave the Seagulls a final first division standing of 13th – the club's best-ever finish.

TUESDAY 16th MAY 1967

The youngest-ever Albion team at this stage in the club's history – average age 21 years and 300 days – faced Doncaster Rovers at Belle Vue.

WEDNESDAY 16th MAY 1979

Portland Timbers, despite taking an early lead, are brushed aside as Albion continued their USA tour with a 2-1 victory in Oregon.

SUNDAY 16th MAY 2004

The first leg of the second division play-off semi-final at the County Ground, Swindon. It was a tight, nervous affair, with neither side wanting to lose, but with 17 minutes remaining Chris Iwelumo won the ball inside the penalty box and passed back to substitute Gary Hart. The utility man spotted midfielder Richard Carpenter in space, who then smashed a trademark long-range effort into the goal in front of the Albion's travelling support to give the Seagulls the advantage going into the second leg at Withdean...

TUESDAY 17th MAY 1966

Police reinforcements were called to the Goldstone to stop youths behind the goal throwing orange peel and whistling during the reserve game against Notts County.

TUESDAY 17th MAY 1977

Albion recorded a 5-3 friendly victory over a Rediffusion All-Star XI, which included manager Alan Mullery, to inaugurate the new floodlights at Worthing Football Club's Woodside Road.

TUESDAY 18th 1954

Albion legend Jimmy Case was born in Liverpool. Pat Saward tried to sign the midfielder as early as 1971. After winning four league titles, one UEFA Cup, one League Cup and three European Cups, Jimmy arrived on the south coast for £350,000 in August 1981. After starring in the FA Cup run of 1983, and an outstanding 1983/84, Case was deemed surplus to requirements and sold to Southampton for £30,000 in March 1985. The Liverpudlian made over 200 first division appearances for Saints before amazingly returning to the Goldstone as a 40-year-old in 1993.

SATURDAY 18th MAY 1963

After the worst winter in living memory, the season finally concluded as already relegated Albion drew 0-0 at Wrexham.

WEDNESDAY 18th MAY 1983

Jimmy Melia announced his team for the FA Cup Final: Moseley, Ramsey, Pearce, Grealish, Stevens, Gatting, Case, Howlett, Robinson, Smith, Smillie; sub. Ryan.

THURSDAY 19th MAY 1983

Albion players Chris Ramsey, Jimmy Case, Gordon Smith and Perry Digweed appeared on Top of the Pops. The club's record, 'The Boys in the Old Brighton Blue', was ranked 127th in the charts!

SUNDAY 19th MAY 1991

It was a midday kick-off for the Division Two play-off semi-final against Millwall at the Goldstone. Hope faded when Paul Stephenson fired the Lions ahead into a 15th-minute lead, but then Albion got their act together to blitz the Londoners with four goals in under 20 minutes of football. Just before half-time Mark Barham was on the end of a huge hoof forward by Albion keeper Perry Digweed to level the scores. After the break Mike Small fired Albion ahead (53), set up Clive Walker to make it 3-1 (55) and then put through Robert Codner to make it 4-1 on the hour! Before the match, Dean Wilkins was presented with a gift from the match sponsors for his man-of-the-match performance in the vital 2-1 win over Ipswich Town eight days earlier… a kettle.

TUESDAY 20th MAY 1975

Richie 'The Bear' Barker was born in Sheffield. The striker became a fans' favourite during the Gillingham years with his hard work and honest approach to the game.

FRIDAY 20th MAY 1983

The Cup Final party left for the Selsdon Park Hotel, just outside Croydon. The players were entertained by part-time comedian Bob 'The Cat' Bevan, a Crystal Palace fan.

TUESDAY 20th MAY 1986

Dean Saunders bagged his first Wales goals (2) in the 3-0 win over Canada in Vancouver.

WEDNESDAY 20th MAY 1998

'The Albion is an essential part of community life; the club is a source of local pride and enjoyment and provides a common bond for the people of Brighton, Hove and much of Sussex. They need to be back in the Brighton area and if they were to disappear it would be a tragedy for the whole of the county.' The conclusion of a statement from the local Green Party supporting the use of Withdean by the Albion.

THURSDAY 20th MAY 2004

Swindon Town were the Withdean visitors for the second leg of the second division play-offs. Richard Carpenter had scored the only goal of the contest at the County Ground just four days earlier. Robins leading scorer Sam Parkin ended Ben Roberts's impressive run of clean sheets by netting just nine minutes from the end of normal time. Substitute Rory Fallon gave the visitors the lead seven minutes into extra time. Albion pushed and pushed but, with leading goalscorer Leon Knight off injured, couldn't convert their chances. As the match entered its final minute, the Wiltshire fans began to celebrate… Charlie Oatway's throw was flicked on by captain Danny Cullip and Adam Virgo threw himself at the ball to force a header past the opposing keeper to send Withdean into raptures. Penalties. Tommy Mooney saw his kick brilliantly saved by Roberts to earn Mark McGhee's men a trip to the Millennium Stadium.

WEDNESDAY 21st MAY 1980

Albion announced a 33 per cent rise in terrace admission prices at the Goldstone – from £1.50 to £2.

SATURDAY 21st MAY 1983

An unforgettable day in the club's history; Brighton & Hove Albion versus Manchester United in the FA Cup Final at Wembley Stadium in front of 100,000 fans and many millions more worldwide on TV. The team flew into north London courtesy of a British Caledonian (the club's sponsor) helicopter. Tony Grealish led the team out, sporting a white headband in sympathy for the suspended Steve Foster – Albion even went to the High Court in an attempt to have Foster's suspension for too many bookings revoked, but failed. The game started well for Albion: on 13 minutes, Gary Howlett floated a cross into the box for Gordon Smith to head into the bottom of the net. One-nil Albion in the Cup Final! In the second half Chris Ramsey was injured by Norman Whiteside and forced off, but not before Frank Stapleton had equalised with Ramsey limping behind him. Ray Wilkins curled a delightful shot around Graham Moseley but hadn't reckoned on Gary Stevens. The man-of-the-match equalised four minutes from the final whistle, firing in from a short corner. In the very last minute of extra-time, Michael Robinson shrugged off Kevin Moran and passed across the box to Gordon Smith. BBC Radio 2 Commentator Peter Jones famously screamed "...and Smith must score" – but United's South African goalkeeper Gary Bailey saved the Scotsman's low shot with his legs. The final whistle blew 21 seconds later... Both teams enjoyed a lap of honour before the Albion flew back to Hove in their helicopter.

SATURDAY 21st MAY 1988

Steve Penney netted the second and last of his international goals for Northern Ireland in the 3-0 win over Malta in Belfast.

MONDAY 21st MAY 1990

Dean Wilkins, trialist Oke Foloronso, Lee Cormack, Garry Nelson, Derek McGrath and Kevin Bremner all hit the target in a 6-0 defeat of Dinamo Moscow reserves in the third and final game of a post-season tour of the USSR.

TUESDAY 22nd MAY 1979

Gerry Ryan scored in his second Republic of Ireland appearance, a 1-1 Dublin draw with West Germany.

WEDNESDAY 22nd MAY 1991

Albion travelled to the Lions' Den. After a resounding 4-1 first leg home play-off victory against Millwall, over 3,000 Albion fans were in South London dreaming of Wembley. An early home strike gave the travelling army the jitters, until Robert Codner buried the equaliser. Young substitute John Robinson replaced Garry Nelson and confirmed the Albion victory with a fine effort. On arrival back in Brighton, the players celebrate at the Event, West Street, where Radio One DJ Bruno Brookes is performing in aid of both Steve Gatting's testimonial and Sussex cricketer Tony Pigott's benefit year.

SATURDAY 23rd MAY 1981

A 3-0 defeat in Poland marked Mark Lawrenson's 14th and final appearance for the Republic of Ireland as an Albion player. The Preston-born defender would go on to win 39 caps for his country, scoring on five occasions.

MONDAY 23rd MAY 1983

There were ugly scenes at the Goldstone Ground as Cup Final Replay tickets go on sale to non-season ticket holders. Trouble flared when fans learned they were restricted to just one ticket each for the match with Manchester United at Wembley.

THURSDAY 24th MAY 1956

Doug Rougvie was born in Fife, Scotland. The uncompromising defender joined for £50,000 from Chelsea in 1987 after winning seven trophies in seven seasons at Aberdeen. The big Scot made 46 appearances, netted three times and captained the club during the 1987/88 promotion season.

WEDNESDAY 24th MAY 2000

On loan from Fulham for the last three months of the previous season, Albion boss Micky Adams signed 23-year-old winger Paul Brooker for £25,000 from the London club.

TUESDAY 25th MAY 1982

England kept a clean sheet in the 2-0 Wembley win over the Netherlands. Albion's Steve Foster gave a solid performance in the centre of defence.

MONDAY 25th MAY 1953

Albion played outside England and Wales for the first time: a 4-4 draw against Belgian side FC Liege. The teams exchanged tie-pins and cuff-links before the kick-off.

THURSDAY 26th MAY 1983

A game Albion fans want to forget; the FA Cup Final replay. On 22 minutes Bryan Robson scored United's first; Norman Whiteside made it 2-0 four minutes later. Albion best chance came when Jimmy Case's shot was deflected, but Gary Bailey managed to tip it over. Robson scored again just before the break and Arnold Muhren added a fourth goal from the penalty spot. The spirit of the Albion fans was never broken as they out-sang the United masses – but Robson lifted the Cup for the Red Devils.

WEDNESDAY 26th MAY 1999

Skint Records, home to Fatboy Slim (Brighton fan Norman Cook), were revealed as Albion's new shirt sponsors. The new kit was manufactured in Italy by Parma-based company Errea.

SATURDAY 27th MAY 1911

Albion were registered at Companies House. The company was listed at 129 Church Road, Hove. The club's Articles of Association did not allow any member of the board to receive any remuneration, and included a clause forbidding any board member to make any financial gain should the club fold. The clause was infamously removed by chairman Bill Archer and Greg Stanley when the pair bought the club for just £100 in 1995.

THURSDAY 27th MAY 1982

Tony Grealish was on the wrong end of a 7-0 scoreline in Brazil. It was the Republic of Ireland midfielder's fourth international appearance while at the Goldstone.

THURSDAY 28th MAY 1998

"When I left in 1981 the club was thriving. That has totally gone and that is why it is so important that we get back to Withdean," declared Albion boss Brian Horton on signing a one-year contract.

MONDAY 28th MAY 1978

Albion were forced to play a fun game, which they won 4-2, with a scratch side of local 'ex-pats' in San Diego. The club had struggled to arrange fixtures on their post-season holiday on the US West Coast due to the fuel crisis.

THURSDAY 29th MAY 1997

Crawley's Broadfield Stadium, Coral's Hove Greyhound Stadium or Gillingham's Priestfield? No decision had been made on where Albion would play home games next season.

WEDNESDAY 30th MAY 1979

Nottingham Forest beat Malmo 1-0 in the European Cup Final in Munich. The manager of both clubs had an Albion connection: the English side's boss was Brian Clough who sat in the Goldstone hotseat for just nine months from November 1973; the Swedish side's gaffer Bob Houghton was with Albion in 1969/70 but never played.

FRIDAY 30th MAY 1997

A very sad day: 95 years after moving into the Goldstone Ground, the club's staff left the premises for the last time.

SUNDAY 30th MAY 2004

The Seagulls headed to Cardiff to face Bristol City in the second division play-off final. Pint-sized hitman Leon Knight – the Second Divison's leading goalscorer – hit the bar with a first-half free-kick but made no mistake from the spot in the 84th minute. Manager Mark McGhee sent out the unused substitutes – Kerry Mayo, Michel Kuipers and Adam Hinshelwood – to warm up with instructions to gee up the fans. Just a few moments later striker Chris Iwelumo played a one-two with Knight and was fouled. Knight converted the kick, to send the 30,000 Seagulls fans into raptures and the team into the Championship!

SUNDAY 31st MAY 1970

Ian Chapman was born in Brighton. The left-back made his debut on Valentine's Day 1987 as a 16-year-old.

SATURDAY 31st MAY 1980

Peter Ward came on in the 85th minute of England's 2-1 win over Australia in Sydney – the shortest-ever international career for an England player.

TUESDAY 31st MAY 2005

Lifelong fan Aaron Berry won the Albion a £250,000 transfer kitty after winning the 'Win A Player' promotion, run by Football League sponsors Coca-Cola. The IT trainer from Worthing registered his vote via the club website every day throughout the 80-day promotion to see off competition from thousands of supporters of Football League and Scottish Premier League clubs. Manager Mark McGhee spent part of the money on Bury's 18-year-old striker Colin Kazim-Richards.

Brighton & Hove Albion

ON THIS DAY

JUNE

SATURDAY 1st JUNE 1940

Albion's only game on this date was a wartime match against Watford that finished 2-2 in front of just 857 fans at the Goldstone.

SUNDAY 2nd JUNE 1991

The biggest away following in the club's history, around 32,400 Albion fans (out of a total of 59,940), were at Wembley for the second division play-off final. Wearing another infamous red and white away kit, the club's third Wembley visit ended in a 3-1 defeat to Notts County.

MONDAY 2nd JUNE 1997

The bulldozers moved in to begin the demolition of the 96-year-old Goldstone Football Ground.

SUNDAY 3rd JUNE 1979

Alan Mullery was sent off during a friendly game against San Diego Sockers in California! One of the home players kicked Peter Sayer and the ex-England captain ran on to the pitch to protest and swore at the officials. He was also later fined £750 and banned from the touchline.

THURSDAY 3rd JUNE 1986

Guadalajara, Mexico, was the setting for Steve Penney's first taste of World Cup action – Northern Ireland drew 1-1 with Algeria.

THURSDAY 4th JUNE 1998

SWEAT (Save Withdean Environment Action Team) rejected Lord Bassam's proposal for the council, club and residents to work together to make the Albion's time at Withdean a success.

MONDAY 5th JUNE 2006

The Seagulls Party was born. Registered with The Electoral Commission, the party would field candidates at future elections and champion the proposed new stadium at Falmer.

TUESDAY 6th JUNE 2000

Adam Virgo, a 17-year-old defender on a scholarship at Ardingly College, signed professional forms in 2000 to follow in his brother's footsteps. James Virgo was an Albion pro from 1995 for two years.

MONDAY 7th JUNE 1986

Spain got their revenge for Northern Ireland's victory four years earlier. Albion's Steve Penney did his best but the red & yellows triumph 2-1 in Guadalajara, Mexico.

TUESDAY 8th JUNE 1948

After finishing bottom of the third division (south), Albion applied for re-election. Chairman Charles Wakeling highlighted ground improvements (extended terracing and an enlarged South Stand) and described the large Goldstone crowds in a letter to the other clubs. Albion received 47 votes, Norwich City 47, Colchester United 2, Gillingham 1 and Worcester City 1.

WEDNESDAY 9th JUNE 1999

David Cameron arrived after buying himself out of the Argyll & Sutherland Highlanders. Once called "useless" by assistant manager Alan Cork and occasionally "silky" by supporters, the striker donned the stripes 17 times without scoring.

TUESDAY 10th JUNE 1947

Jim Walker was born in Northwich, Cheshire. The midfielder was signed from Derby County by Peter Taylor but never lived up to his £25,000 price tag and left for Peterborough United after two Hove years in 1976.

SATURDAY 11th JUNE 1988

After the fantastic promotion run-in, 1,500 Albion fans wasted no time in snapping up season tickets for the new second division campaign.

THURSDAY 11th JUNE 1998

One of the best bits of transfer business in the history of the Albion; warehouseman Gary Hart arrived from Essex League Stansted for just £1,000 and a playing kit. Originally signed as a striker, the popular player has featured in many positions in his 300-plus Albion appearances.

FRIDAY 12th JUNE 1981

Alan Mullery, the club's most successful manager ever, shocked the football world by resigning as Albion boss.

WEDNESDAY 13th JUNE 1973

The club lost one of its favourite sons; Charlie Webb passed away in Hove aged 86. Such was the inside-left's love of the Albion that he turned down a chance to manage Tottenham Hotspur before World War II.

THURSDAY 14th JUNE 1905

One-season wonder Hugh Vallance was born in Wolverhampton. The striker scored an amazing 30 league goals in just 37 third division (south) games in the 1929/30 season, one more than team-mate Dan Kirkwood.

MONDAY 15th JUNE 1998

Albion appointed Martin Hinshelwood as director of youth, a day before his birthday, together with Dean Wilkins as youth team coach.

MONDAY 16th JUNE 1997

Spokesman for the new incoming board, and future chief executive, Martin Perry tells fans he is confident the £500,000 bond required for Albion to remain in the Football League and play their football at Gillingham would be lodged within the five-day deadline.

SATURDAY 16th JUNE 2001

Albion congregated at St. Peter's Church, Brighton, to celebrate the club's 100th anniversary at a special thanksgiving service. The building was decked in blue and white balloons for the occasion. Brighton and Hove mayor Harry Steer declared: "God bless you Albion, from the city of Brighton and Hove we congratulate you on your centenary and we wish you every success in the future, going up and up."

SATURDAY 17th JUNE 1911

Don Barker was born in Derbyshire. The inside-forward was signed as a 35-year-old by Charlie Webb for £400 in July 1946 and had to travel to home matches from his Midlands home due to the lack of housing in Sussex at the time.

THURSDAY 18th JUNE 1931

Peter Harburn was born in Finsbury, London. The striker scored 65 goals in 133 starts before an £8,000 move to first division Everton in 1958.

FRIDAY 19th JUNE 1931

The founder of Brighton & Hove Albion Football Club, John Jackson, died at the age of 70. The son of a Birmingham master toolmaker, John represented Coventry Rangers between the sticks, then coached at Liverpool and Leicester Fosse before arriving on the south coast.

WEDNESDAY 20th JUNE 1951

Billy McEwan was born in Lanarkshire, Scotland. The midfielder began his career at Hibernian before heading south to Blackpool in May 1973 and then completing his journey in that direction when Brian Clough signed him for £15,000 in February 1974. Despite only making 28 appearances – scoring three times – Billy showed great leadership qualities, which stood in him good stead for a later managerial career.

MONDAY 21st JUNE 1999

Paul Watson and Charlie Oatway arrived from Brentford for a joint fee of £30,000. Albion also announced a £1 million investment from Derek Chapman, chairman of the Adenstar group which rebuilt Withdean, and an anonymous benefactor (later revealed as Kevin Griffiths).

SUNDAY 21st JUNE 1964

Swansea is the setting for the birth of Dean Saunders. The Welsh striker began his career at the Vetch Field but was released in July 1985. He arrived in Hove and quickly impressed the Goldstone fans with his pace and eye for goal. After netting 19 times in his first season Saunders' form dipped and he was sold to Oxford United.

MONDAY 22nd JUNE 1998

The club announced a novel, free travel zone extending throughout the Brighton and Hove area. A travel voucher would be included with each match ticket to be exchanged for free bus or train travel to Withdean.

TUESDAY 23rd JUNE 1998

Paul Holsgrove joined on a free transfer from Stoke City and signs a two-year contract. The 28-year-old midfielder would prove to be one of the biggest bargains in the club's history – despite not playing a single competitive game – when he was sold to Hibernian just six weeks later for £110,000!

MONDAY 24th JUNE 1901

The day the Albion was born! Brighton & Hove Albion Football Club came into being on this very day at the Seven Stars Public House in Ship Street, Brighton. John Jackson – who had previously been involved with Brighton United – was hoping it would be third time lucky this time around for a Brighton football team (there had also been Brighton & Hove Rangers). The new club was to be christened Brighton & Hove United but Hove Football Club objected on the grounds that they would lose support as the public may assume United are a merger of the former United and Rangers. As a result the Albion was born. The origins of the name are unclear but two reasons stand out: the town had many businesses with the Albion suffix, or may have been that founder Jackson had close links with West Bromwich Albion.

SUNDAY 24th JUNE 2001

Brighton & Hove Albion Football Club celebrated their one hundredth birthday on this day. During that time the club had won the Charity Shield in 1910, been elected to the Football League, enjoyed eleven promotions and suffered nine relegations.

TUESDAY 25th JUNE 1982

It was a great day for the Albion. Sammy Nelson came on against Spain in the famous 1-0 World Cup win for Northern Ireland over the hosts in Valencia. The crucial goal was scored by Gerry Armstrong, who would go on to play for the Albion a few years later. Nearly 300 miles away in Bilbao, Steve Foster made his third and last England appearance in the 1-0 win over Kuwait.

MONDAY 25th JUNE 2007

Nicky Forster joined the Albion from Hull City in a £75,000 deal. The 33 year-old forward scored 146 league goals in 488 appearances for Ipswich Town, Reading, Birmingham City, Brentford and Gillingham.

WEDNESDAY 26th JUNE 1974

Former Dutch marine Michel Kuipers was born in Amsterdam. After just one appearance for Bristol Rovers, Micky Adams picked up the big keeper on a free transfer in June 2000. Capable of world-class saves, the Dutchman is a crowd favourite.

THURSDAY 27th JUNE 2002

The Society of Sussex Downsmen, the oldest conservation group in the South Downs, called for a public inquiry into the plans for a new stadium at Falmer.

FRIDAY 27th JUNE 2003

An Albion All-Stars team beat Southampton 7-6 at the Pro-Beach Soccer Kronenbourg Cup. John Byrne hit a hat-trick, captain Dean Wilkins scored two, Bob Booker got another and Paul Rogers scored the fifth on a pitch made from over 400 tonnes of imported sand.

WEDNESDAY 28th JUNE 1933

A future Busby Babe was born in Lancashire. Freddie Goodwin first came to prominence at Manchester United in 1953 but was overshadowed by the outstanding Duncan Edwards, who sadly died in the Munich air crash of 1958. After a spell with Leeds United, and short tenures at Scunthorpe United and New York Generals, Freddie took control in Hove in November 1968, transforming a relegation-threatened side into promotion chasers. Freddie left for Birmingham City in May 1970.

FRIDAY 29th JUNE 2001

Albion agreed compensation from big-spending Cardiff City for the shock departure of former assistant Alan Cork.

SATURDAY 29th JUNE 2002

Former Stoke City and Icelandic international boss Gudjon Thordarson declared his intention to apply for the Albion manager's job.

FRIDAY 30th JUNE 2006

The Argus reported that the war medals of former Albion chairman Captain William Charles 'Carlo' Campbell were to be auctioned. He was decorated for gallantry while flying more than 20 sorties within a few months during the First World War but was best known for an abortive bid to bring cheetah racing to Britain in 1937. He imported six cheetahs to perk up greyhound racing at the White City greyhound track in west London but the 70mph creatures failed to muster the necessary competitive spirit. An observer recalled that "they just wandered about".

Brighton & Hove Albion
ON THIS DAY

JULY

MONDAY 1st JULY 1996

Out-of-contract skipper Paul McCarthy signed for Wycombe Wanderers for a fee that was eventually set by a tribunal at £100,000. The 24-year-old Irishman made 217 appearances for the Albion and scored eight times.

MONDAY 2nd JULY 1928

Peter Taylor, the first Albion-related one, was born in Nottingham. He met Brian Clough while at Middlesbrough in the 1950s and the pair's careers were linked for the next 27 years. They arrived at the Goldstone in late 1973; Clough would depart just eight months later, but Taylor honoured his contract and signed two of the club's all-time great players for ridiculously low fees; Brian Horton for £27,000 and Peter Ward for just £4,000! He rejoined his old friend in 1976 and the two would lead Forest to a league title and two successive European Cup triumphs.

MONDAY 2nd JULY 2001

Jimmy Collins recalled his playing days. "I'm a nice man, but I had a bad attitude during my time as a player which I regret," said the man who led Albion to the fourth division title in 1965. "I had two or three fights; one was with Jimmy Cooper, another with Wally Gould. I also had one with Tony Marchi when I was at Spurs. They all occurred during five-a-sides. I had a bit of a temper."

TUESDAY 3rd JULY 1883

The first player to score 50 goals for the club, Jack Hall, was born in Hucknall, Nottinghamshire. The centre-forward signed for Albion from Stoke City in 1906 and his prolific form – 54 goals in 93 starts – attracted the attention of first division Middlesbrough in 1908.

SATURDAY 3rd JULY 1937

Frank Scott, who became the first regular goalscorer for Albion on his arrival at the Goldstone in 1902, died in Lincoln. The centre-forward netted 34 times in just 50 appearances.

FRIDAY 4th JULY 1997

The scene of many ups, downs, lows and fantastic highs, the Goldstone Ground is finally demolished. The work, which took five weeks, razed the 96-year-old football arena to the ground, making way for a retail park.

FRIDAY 5th JULY 1957

Chris Hutchings, who made 175 appearances for the Albion, was born in Winchester. The defender-cum-midfielder was once arrested by Hove Police, while playing for Chelsea in the London club's first league visit to the Goldstone Ground in September 1983. In a match that saw a riot by visiting Chelsea fans, Hutchings – the opposing left-back – swore at a policeman who asked him to leave the pitch. By the time he stood before Hove magistrates he had signed for the Albion!

MONDAY 5th JULY 1999

The South Stand seating arrives at Withdean – 19 days before the first scheduled match at the stadium, a friendly against Nottingham Forest.

THURSDAY 6th JULY 1876

An eventual Celtic Park favourite, Paddy Gilhooly was born in Scotland. The inside-right was brought to the Goldstone in 1904 after a three-year spell at White Hart Lane and, previously, a successful campaign in Glasgow. Paddy was released in 1905 after scoring five times in 16 starts. He sadly died two years later, aged just 31.

TUESDAY 7th JULY 1931

Alex South was born in Brighton. The centre-half played for Whitehawk Boys Club before joining the Goldstone ground staff. The local lad made 85 starts in eight years.

MONDAY 7th JULY 2000

Dick Knight appeared on TalkSport's 'From the Boardroom' radio show to answer questions from supporters. The chairman revealed that Falmer would cost more than £40 million, £10 million of which would be spent on infrastructure, but he hoped that one day it might host a World Cup game. In five years' time, Knight said he saw the club playing at Falmer, possibly playing in front of regular crowds of 20,000 in the first division.

WEDNESDAY 8th JULY 1931

Outside-right Bobby Farrell – who would go on to score 95 goals in 466 Albion appearances – picked up a receipt for his wages of £8.

WEDNESDAY 8th JULY 1959

FA Cup Final left-back Graham Pearce was born in Hammersmith, London. Just nine months before the big day out at Wembley, the defender was plying his trade with non-league Barnet. Mike Bailey paid £20,000 for Pearce, an understudy to Sammy Nelson and Steve Gatting, in 1982. A series of injuries saw the stocky Londoner runout on 21st May 1983.

FRIDAY 8th JULY 1977

Albion paid Preston North End £111,111 for the services of central defender Mark Lawrenson. At the time it was the record transfer fee paid out by the club – and certainly proves money well spent as Lawrenson is sold to Liverpool for £900,000 four years later.

MONDAY 8th JULY 2002

Chief executive Martin Perry declared that Arsenal stalwart Tony Adams will not be taking over as Albion manager.

FRIDAY 9th JULY 1999

Manager Micky Adams took his squad to Ballygar in County Galway, Ireland. The pre-season 'bonding' trip included a number of newcomers including Paul Watson, Paul Rogers, Ryan Palmer, Jamie Campbell and Charlie Oatway – plus triallists Chris Wilder and Aidan Newhouse.

WEDNESDAY 10th JULY 2002

Albion joined fellow Football League clubs in a mass protest over the collapsed ITV Digital deal. Representatives of almost all of the 72 league clubs picketed outside the London offices of Carlton and Granada, the parent companies behind the defunct channel. The protest raised awareness of the High Court battle to recoup the £178.5million lost.

MONDAY 11th JULY 1988

Former chairman Mike Bamber died after a two-year battle with cancer. Bamber joined the board in 1970 and became chairman three years later. In November 1973 he persuaded Brian Clough – who always regarded Bamber as the best chairman he worked for – to take over the reins but it was his appointment of Alan Mullery in 1976 that paved the way for the club's golden years.

THURSDAY 12th JULY 1962

Dean Wilkins was born in Middlesex. The midfielder joined the Albion after making two appearances for Queens Park Rangers in 1983 but soon departed for PEC Zwolle in Holland – on the recommendation of Hans Kraay – for three years. The 25-year-old returned in 1987 when Barry Lloyd paid £10,000 for his services. Wilkins became an integral part of the promotion side in 1988 and the play-off final losing team of 1991 – making 123 consecutive appearances – with his incisive passing and creativity. Dean rejoined Albion – after 375 appearances and 31 goals – as youth team coach in 1998 and took over as first-team boss in September 2006.

THURSDAY 12th JULY 2001

There was a huge response to the proposal by Brighton & Hove Albion to build a community stadium on land at Falmer. More than 4,500 fans wrote to the City Council asking it to keep the Falmer site in its 'Local Plan'. But roughly the same number, spurred on by environmentalists and Falmer Parish Council, were against the idea.

MONDAY 13th JULY 1987

Barry Lloyd sold skipper Danny Wilson to Luton Town for £150,000. New centre-half Doug Rougvie replaced the Northern Ireland international as the club's new captain.

SATURDAY 14th JULY 1979

Alan Mullery paid a club record £250,000 for Aston Villa right-back John Gregory.

WEDNESDAY 14th JULY 1999

New striker David Cameron, who had bought himself out of the Army to become a professional footballer, impressed in the victory over Saltdean United. The Scot was not allowed to travel with the first team on the pre-season tour of Ireland because of defence regulations.

SUNDAY 15th JULY 1928

The day Jimmy Leadbetter was born in Edinburgh. The inside-forward had a tough job following in the footsteps of Johnny McNichol but managed a highly credible 33 goals in 133 Albion starts.

FRIDAY 16th JULY 1976

Manager Peter Taylor resigned. He was replaced by former England star
Alan Mullery who had no previous managerial experience. Chairman
Mike Bamber later reveals he thought Mullery would make a good
boss when he saw him thump a team-mate while playing for Fulham.

WEDNESDAY 16th JULY 1997

A meeting between Dick Knight and Bill Archer produced an agreed
timetable to the change in ownership of the club. The proposed ground-
share with Millwall was not sanctioned so Gillingham's Priestfield
Stadium would be 'home' for the next two years.

WEDNESDAY 17th JULY 1901

Despite the Albion's founders persuading Hove FC that they would
not use the 'United' suffix for their new club – so as not to confuse locals
who might assume the new club was an amalgamation – the Goldstone
Ground's owners still threatened to get the FA involved.

MONDAY 18th JULY 1983

The British press reported the Albion are to sign…Kevin Keegan!
The pint-sized striker ended up at Newcastle United. Seafront Rock
Shop owner Chris Cattlin took over from Jimmy Melia – who was on
holiday and knew nothing of the appointment – at the Goldstone.

SATURDAY 18th JULY 1987

After seven years of all-blue shirts Albion announce the return to the
famous blue and white stripes.

FRIDAY 18th JULY 2003

Goalscoring machine Bobby Zamora was sold to Tottenham Hotspur
for a club record fee of £1.5 million. Despite its inevitability, the sale
devastated Albion fans.

SUNDAY 19th JULY 1953

Malcolm Poskett was born in Middlesbrough. The striker worked on the
North Sea oil rigs before re-joining Hartlepool in 1978. Alan Mullery
shelled out £60,000 in the same year and, despite competition from Teddy
Maybank and Peter Ward, he hit 18 goals in 51 games for Albion.

SATURDAY 19th JULY 1958

FA Cup Finalist Neil Smillie was born in Yorkshire. The winger played a key role on the road to Wembley and scored three times in 98 appearances before a £100,000 switch to Watford in 1985.

MONDAY 20th JULY 1964

A man synonymous with his birthplace, Steve Cotterill was born in Cheltenham. First division Wimbledon shelled out £60,000 to prise the goalscorer away from Burton Albion in 1989. Hampered by injuries, the forward managed only 17 league starts in four seasons before joining Albion on a two-month loan for the start of the 1994/95 campaign. He formed a useful partnership with Paul Moulden and netted four times in 11 appearances.

SATURDAY 20th JULY 1974

Leeds United manager Don Revie was appointed England boss. The Elland Road outfit announce their new manager as Brian Clough. Only problem is that the outspoken former goal machine is in charge at the Albion! Chairman Mike Bamber agreed compensation of £75,000 for the remaining four years of his manager's contract, but Leeds reneged on the original deal and eventually paid Albion £45,000. Clough lasted 44 days in West Yorkshire.

WEDNESDAY 20th JULY 2005

Celtic manager Gordon Strachan paid £1.5 million for Albion utility man and reigning player-of-the-season Adam Virgo. Played as a centre-back or centre-forward his nine goals the previous season help the Seagulls retain their place in the Championship.

WEDNESDAY 21st JULY 2004

Former Atletico Madrid reserve Maheta Molango signs for Albion – after netting three times in two trial games – with a warning from Mark McGhee. "We will wait until we've got him signed and sealed before we reveal details like the length of contract," declared the Scot.

FRIDAY 22nd JULY 1983

Albion's shirt sponsors, British Caledonian Airways, pulled out of the deal after three years.

TUESDAY 23rd JULY 1974

Leeds United claimed it was, in fact, Brian Clough who had asked to be taken on at Elland Road and not the other way round.

FRIDAY 23rd JULY 1999

The safety certificate for Withdean was granted at 5.30 pm, the day before the first Albion game there; a friendly against Nottingham Forest.

TUESDAY 24th JULY 1984

Mike Bamber's reign as Albion chairman came to an end after 11 tumultuous years. Disillusioned directors – not happy with Bamber's running of the club – appoint Brian Bedson as chairman.

SATURDAY 24th JULY 1999

After two long years at Gillingham, Albion are finally back in Brighton. The Withdean welcomed Nottingham Forest for the inaugural friendly match. Albion's players arrived on an open-top bus, while the Brighton Silver Band played 'Sussex by the Sea' as the teams ran out in front of the sell-out 5,891 crowd. There was a streaker (male) during the 2-2 draw, Gary Hart scored the first Withdean goal, and the first of hundreds of supporters' litter patrols began in earnest.

THURSDAY 24th JULY 2003

Albion boss Steve Coppell signed striker Leon Knight from Chelsea on a two-month loan deal.

TUESDAY 24th JULY 2007

Secretary of State for Communities and Local Government Hazel Blears gave the community stadium at Falmer planning approval. Following public inquiries, the then-deputy Prime Minister John Prescott initially approved the plans back in October 2005 before Lewes District Council, among others, announced it would appeal against the decision on planning grounds. Over 10 years since a ball was last kicked at the Goldstone Ground, Albion finally looked set to have a home of their own. Manager Dean Wilkins summed up the decision: "I'm so pleased for the supporters who have had the unfortunate situation of travelling to Gillingham for two years and then being stuck at Withdean for such a long time. I am absolutely thrilled for them."

FRIDAY 25th JULY 1969

Due to the lack of pitches in Spain, Albion went on a three-match tour of the Republic of Ireland instead. Alex Dawson (2) and Allan Gilliver scored the goals for Freddie Goodwin's men in the 3-0 win at Dundalk.

FRIDAY 26th JULY 1996

Albion defensive colossus Steve Foster – 1979 to 1984 and 1992 to 1995 – enjoyed a testimonial at the Goldstone Ground. The game was rescheduled from the end of the previous season after the pitch invasion against York City.

THURSDAY 26th JULY 2007

Albion spent just £13,600 on agents' fees in the period between 1st January and 30th June, and £51,100 for the year. The figures were included in the Agents' Fees report, regularly released by the Football League.

WEDNESDAY 27th JULY 1955

A true Albion legend was born in Lichfield, Staffordshire. Considered too small to be a professional footballer, Peter Ward began an apprenticeship as an engine-fitter at Rolls Royce. The forward eventually arrived on the south coast after netting 21 goals in 50 games for Burton Albion. In 1975 their manager Ken Guttridge became assistant to Peter Taylor, who gambled £4,000 on the slight striker. Wardy scored within 50 seconds of his Albion debut and set the scene for a scintillating Albion career. Pacy dribbling, speed off the mark and the ability to turn on a sixpence lit up the Goldstone in the late 70s. Average crowds of over 23,000 witnessed some great football as Albion rose from the third to first division. Wardy broke the club's season goalscoring record with 36 in 1976/77 and netted 16 in the club's inaugural top-flight campaign in 1979/80. In October 1980, the 25-year-old joined former boss Peter Taylor at Nottingham Forest for £450,000 as part of the transfer triangle that took Garry Birtles to Manchester United and Andy Ritchie to the south coast.

WEDNESDAY 27th JULY 2005

Mark McGhee told *The Argus* that new Argentinean centre-forward Federico Turienzo could be Albion's answer to Peter Crouch. The 6ft 3ins 22-year-old started just one game and failed to find the net.

MONDAY 29th JULY 2002

Marijan Kovacevic enjoyed his first taste of English football, partnering captain Danny Cullip in the centre of defence in this pre-season friendly at Leyton Orient. Jamaican culinary queen Rusty Lee was in the main stand with husband Andreas Hohmann, the Croatian trialist's agent.

FRIDAY 30th JULY 1915

George Curtis's successor was born in Falkirk, Scotland. Archie Macaulay, one of the best-known names in 40s and 50s football, took charge of the Albion in April 1963. The Scot enjoyed an illustrious playing career. He won a Scottish League title with Rangers in 1935, represented his country, and gained a first division championship medal with Arsenal, aged 32, in 1948. Responsible for the signing of Bobby Smith, Archie spent five-and-a-half years at the Goldstone but couldn't quite achieve promotion to the second tier.

THURSDAY 30th JULY 1998

The battle to 'Bring Home the Albion' took another twist. SWEAT had filed papers in the High Court seeking a judicial review into the council's decision to grant Albion planning permission.

TUESDAY 31st JULY 1979

Albion launched the club's first standing season ticket. Priced at £31.50 for the first division debut campaign, they were initially confined to the south-eastern corner of the Goldstone terraces.

TUESDAY 31st JULY 2007

Lewes District Council announced it was not going to appeal the Government's decision to allow Albion's new stadium to be built at Falmer. The council released a statement saying it was frustrated and alarmed at the "blatantly party-political" decision to award planning consent but for "practical reasons" had decided not to appeal.

Brighton & Hove Albion
ON THIS DAY

AUGUST

THURSDAY 1st AUGUST 1968

Albion ventured over the Scottish border for the first time. The short tour of northern England and Scotland included a goal from Paul Flood in a 1-1 draw with Falkirk.

TUESDAY 1st AUGUST 1978

Chris Iwelumo was born in Coatbridge – home of Albion Rovers – in Scotland. The big striker netted four times in 10 loan appearances in 2004. The 6ft 4ins hitman was fouled for the penalty that Leon Knight converted in the 2004 play-off final against Bristol City.

MONDAY 2nd AUGUST 1937

Adrian Thorne was born in Hove. The forward waited over three years to make his debut and eventually appeared for the first team while stationed in Colchester during his Army national service. On only his 17th league outing, the local lad banged in five goals against Watford! The attacker went on to score 44 times in 84 Albion starts in four seasons but never really had the opportunity to establish himself. He moved to Plymouth Argyle in 1961, Exeter City in 1963 and finally, in the league, Leyton Orient in 1965.

SATURDAY 2nd AUGUST 1997

Albion's first 'home' game at Gillingham was a friendly 1-1 draw with Crystal Palace in front of only 652 fans, around 200 of whom had made the soon-to-be-all-too-familiar journey from Sussex.

WEDNESDAY 2nd AUGUST 2000

A historic day for the Albion; Brighton & Hove Council allocated land in its 'Draft Deposit Local Plan' for a new stadium: at Village Way North, near Falmer. The development would start with a 10,000-seat West Stand and a temporary 4,000-seat East Stand. A permanent East Stand, then South and North Stands, would follow at a later date, giving a final capacity of 22,438 seats.

MONDAY 3rd AUGUST 1998

Brian Horton's Albion beat Newcastle Town – in a game sponsored by the Church of Scientology – and won 3-0 thanks to goals from Kerry Mayo, Richard Barker and Stafford Browne.

WEDNESDAY 4th AUGUST 1971

An Albion favourite was born in Cork, Republic of Ireland. Paul McCarthy played hurling and Gaelic football at school but was spotted playing football for Rockmount by scout Ted Streeter and came over to England in 1988. The fee was a couple of match balls! After making his debut in 1992, the centre-back was a fixture in the side scoring eight times in 217 Albion appearances before a move to Wycombe Wanderers in 1996 for £100,000.

MONDAY 4th AUGUST 1980

NAC Breda were the opposition for this friendly in Holland. The players left the pitch for 20 minutes during a violent hailstorm.

WEDNESDAY 5th AUGUST 1987

George Graham's Arsenal walloped the Albion 7-2 at the Goldstone Ground in a pre-season friendly. Steve Penney and new striker Kevin Bremner scored the consolation goals for Barry Lloyd's side.

SATURDAY 5th AUGUST 2006

Alex Revell made a scoring debut in the 1-0 League One victory at Rotherham United, on the club's earliest start to a new campaign.

MONDAY 6th AUGUST 1979

The day after the Tennent Caledonian Cup concluded in Glasgow, Albion continued their pre-season in the Netherlands. Following a number of flight cancellations, the team landed just 90 minutes before their game with the East German Olympic Team at Beneden-Leeweden. Peter Ward was sent off after retaliating to some harsh treatment during the 2-0 defeat.

THURSDAY 6th AUGUST 1998

Donatello were announced as the new shirt sponsor after five years of paint manufacturers Sandtex.

SATURDAY 6th AUGUST 2005

Jason Dodd, Wayne Henderson, Paul McShane and Colin Kazim-Richards made their Albion debuts at Derby County's Pride Park. Dean Hammond grabbed an early header in the 1-1 draw. The 1,751 Albion fans present also saw referee Brian Curson limp off injured.

SATURDAY 7th AUGUST 1999

The day Albion fans everywhere had been waiting for; the end of the two-year exile in Gillingham! Mansfield Town were the first visitors to Withdean, the club's new temporary home. Appropriately, six players made their debuts in the 6-0 demolition of the lame Stags; Chris Wilder, Andy Crosby, Charlie Oatway, Jamie Campbell, Paul Rogers, Aidan Newhouse and Darren Freeman. Newhouse grabbed a brace while Freeman helped himself to a hat-trick, the first Albion player to score three times on his debut since the club's very first game in 1901. The majority of the 5,882 fans in attendance went home very happy indeed.

SATURDAY 7th AUGUST 2004

Maheta Molango scored just 12 seconds into his debut for Albion, in a 3-2 defeat at Reading in the Championship. Nicky Forster grabbed the Royals' third on the hour before 17-year-old substitute Jake Robinson struck a delightful consolation shortly after replacing Adam Virgo. Darren Currie, Alexis Nicolas and Albert Jarrett also made their debuts.

MONDAY 8th AUGUST 1955

Albion opened a new ground at Boulivot, in Jersey, by demolishing an island Saturday League XI 15-0!

WEDNESDAY 8th AUGUST 1984

Gerry Ryan made his 14th, and final, Republic of Ireland appearance in the 0-0 stalemate with Mexico in Dublin.

SATURDAY 8th AUGUST 1998

Gary Hart, Mark Walton, the experienced Micky Bennett and former Hastings Town striker Stafford Browne made their Albion debuts in the 1-0 third division defeat at Carlisle United.

WEDNESDAY 9th AUGUST 2000

After scoring six goals in six games while on loan in the previous campaign, Bobby Zamora signed from Bristol Rovers for £100,000, the biggest deal since John Byrne arrived for £125,000 a decade earlier. The 19-year-old penned a four-year contract and chairman Dick Knight said of the deal: "He's an exciting player and the Albion are definitely going to be the team to watch this season."

SATURDAY 10th AUGUST 1968

Lou Haestier hosted the first 'Radio Goldstone' pre-match entertainment programme over the tannoy before the opening day 2-1 third division win over Mansfield Town.

SATURDAY 10th AUGUST 2002

Martin Hinshelwood made a dream start as Albion boss at Turf Moor. The 3-1 first division win over Burnley came courtesy of strikes from Steve Melton, Paul Brooker and Bobby Zamora. The starting line-up – after a virus had swept through the squad – included the manager's 17-year-old nephew Adam on his full league debut, after Danny Cullip was laid low by a virus.

SATURDAY 10th AUGUST 2004

The Albion lost their first home game in the in the Football League's new-look Championship 2-0 to Plymouth Argyle. It's a bad night for defenders Danny Cullip and Dan Harding: the former scores an own goal to give the Pilgrims the lead, while the latter concedes a penalty just before half-time and is shown a red card before Paul Wotton scores from the spot for the visitors.

SATURDAY 11th AUGUST 1951

Before pre-season friendlies became commonplace, Albion used to warm up with public practice matches between two sides of the club's players: the Blues beat the Yellows 6-0.

WEDNESDAY 11th AUGUST 1999

It was a night of firsts at Withdean: the first cup game – in the Worthington Cup – is against former landlords Gillingham and is the first under floodlights. The first goals scored by any away team – two – result in the first-ever defeat at the Albion's new 'temporary' home. Unfortunately, Meridian decide to show extensive highlights of the 2-0 reverse.

SATURDAY 11th AUGUST 2001

Former Fulham captain Simon Morgan made his Albion debut in the opening day 0-0 draw against Cambridge United at the Abbey Stadium. The defender went on to make 42 league appearances during the championship-winning campaign.

MONDAY 12th AUGUST 1946

Fred Binney was born in Plymouth. The prolific striker – 44 goals in 85 games – lost his place to Ian Mellor in 1976 after two great seasons.

SATURDAY 12th AUGUST 2000

Micky Adams' revolution continued as four of his new players – Richard Carpenter, Michel Kuipers, Mark Cartwright and Lee Steele – made their debuts at Southend United. The 3,000-plus Albion fans welcomed their team with a chorus of: 'Bring on the champions'. The inspiring chant had little effect on the result, a 2-0 third division defeat.

SATURDAY 13th AUGUST 1977

John Ruggiero, Eric Potts, Gary Williams and Mark Lawrenson made their Albion debuts in the 0-0 League Cup draw at Cambridge United.

SATURDAY 13th AUGUST 1994

The blue-and-black striped away strip – inspired by manager Liam Brady's association with Internazionale of Milan – was worn at the Vetch Field as Albion fielded two new players, both signed on free transfers from Tottenham Hotspur: Jeff Minton and Junior McDougald. Albion drew 1-1 with the Swans, Cardiff City supporter Kurt Nogan was on target with the goal.

MONDAY 13th AUGUST 2007

Melanie Cuttress, Chairman of Falmer Parish Council, announced "reluctantly" that, following legal advice, they would not challenge the Secretary of State's decision to grant permission for a community stadium at Falmer.

SATURDAY 14th AUGUST 1976

It was Alan Mullery's first competitive game in charge – Southend United away. Experienced defenders Chris Cattlin and Graham Cross made their debut in a match which ended in a 1-1 draw.

SATURDAY 14th AUGUST 1993

The threat of a winding-up order hung over the club as the league campaign kicks off in Bradford. A second division 2-0 defeat to City is notable for the debut of 18-year-old goalkeeper Nicky Rust.

SATURDAY 15th AUGUST 1970

Peter O'Sullivan made his Albion debut in the 0-0 home draw with Torquay United. Joining the club as a 19-year-old, the Welshman graced the left flank with distinction during his 11 years with the club. A full Welsh international, 'Sully' scored 43 goals in 491 appearances.

SATURDAY 15th AUGUST 1981

Republic of Ireland international defender Mark Lawrenson was sold to Liverpool for a club record £900,000.

SATURDAY 15th AUGUST 1992

Loan forwards Steve Cotterill and Paul Moulden both scored on their debuts in Albion's first game in the new Division Two – after the formation of the Premier League – a 3-2 defeat at Leyton Orient.

WEDNESDAY 15th AUGUST 2007

The South Downs Society announced that they would not challenge the government's decision to allow the building of a stadium at Falmer.

SUNDAY 16th AUGUST 1931

Sydney Ellis was born in Charlton, London. The full-back represented London Schools and joined Crystal Palace as an amateur in May 1949. After National Service he played for Charlton and arrived at the Goldstone for £2,000 in 1957. He appeared 44 times in two campaigns.

SATURDAY 16th AUGUST 1980

At the risk of incurring the wrath of many Albion fans, Mike Bamber dispensed with 'Good Old Sussex by the Sea' in favour of 'Gonna Fly Now' the title theme from the film *Rocky*. The chairman was inspired after a visit to San Diego Sockers. New signing Gordon Smith scored the first while John Gregory hit the second in the 2-0 first division Goldstone victory over Wolves. The crowd of 19,307 saw the team run out in all-blue shirts adorned with first-time sponsor British Caledonian.

SATURDAY 16th AUGUST 1997

Albion's first 'home' league game at Gillingham – a 1-1 draw watched by just 2,336 fans – was also Macclesfield Town's first match as new members of the Football League.

Thursday 17th August 1967

John Napier signed for a record fee of £25,000 from Bolton Wanderers. The centre-half was a mainstay in the Albion rearguard for five years. He played on 247 occasions, scoring five times, until moving on to Bradford City for £10,000 in 1972.

Saturday 17th August 1985

Dean Saunders, who would score 25 goals in 86 games, Dennis Mortimer, Justin Fashanu and Gavin Oliver all made their debuts watched by 9,787 Goldstone fans in the 2-2 home draw with Grimsby Town.

Saturday 18th August 1979

Albion's first ever game in the first division was at home to FA Cup holders Arsenal. Unfortunately, the Gunners hadn't read the script as Republic of Ireland international Frank Stapleton, bubble-permed Alan Sunderland (2) and Liam Brady all netted in the 4-0 win. Future Albion players in the Gunners squad included Sammy Nelson, Steve Gatting and Frank Stapleton.

Saturday 18th August 2007

Albion's Withdean victory over Northampton Town was the third successive 2-1 home triumph on this date. In 2001, Wigan Athletic lost in the third division and, two years later, Queens Park Rangers are defeated in the division above.

Wednesday 19th August 1953

An Albion all-time great made his debut in a 2-1 win at Queens Park Rangers. Much-loved left-back Jimmy Langley missed only five games in his four years at the Goldstone. The Londoner thrilled the 1950s crowds with his dribbling and many a tear was shed when Fulham paid £12,000 for his services in 1957, after 16 goals in 178 starts.

Saturday 19th August 1961

George Curtis's first game in charge is a 3-3 draw at Scunthorpe United. Despite signing future club stalwarts Norman Gall, Jimmy Collins and Bill Cassidy, the Essex man's 77-game tenure will be remembered for successive relegations, culminating in a drop to the fourth division in 1963 – confirmed three months after he was released from his contract.

THURSDAY 20th AUGUST 1925

Johnny McNichol was born in Kilmarnock, Scotland. The influential inside-forward signed for a club record £5,000 from Newcastle United and played a pivotal role in the club's resurgence in the late 1940s, early 50s. In 1952 Chelsea paid Albion £12,000, doubling the club's previous record fee received. He had scored 39 times in 165 starts for the Albion, and then while on the books at Stamford Bridge he helped the London club win their first-ever league title in 1955.

SATURDAY 20th AUGUST 1960

Albion lost their season-opener 4-1 at Derby County's Baseball Ground. The club have never won on this date in nine attempts.

SATURDAY 20th AUGUST 1966

Future England manager Howard Wilkinson enjoys a goalscoring debut in the 2-2 draw at Swindon Town in the first of his 147 games for Albion.

WEDNESDAY 20th AUGUST 1986

Albion Lifeline is launched at The Dome. The fund-raising scheme was intended to have 2,500 members who paid a subscription for regular prize draws. The proceeds were initially used to buy a number of players, but the funds were thereafter swallowed up by general costs.

SATURDAY 21st AUGUST 1948

After finishing bottom of the third division South in May, Albion kicked off the new season in all-blue shirts with white sleeves – the first time the stripes had been changed since 1904. Ken Davies, Ron Guttridge, George Lewis – who scored – and Johnny McNichol made their debuts in a 1-1 home draw with Swindon Town. The gate was 21,593.

SATURDAY 21st AUGUST 1999

Left-footed right-back Paul Watson made the first of his 215 Albion appearances in the 1-0 third division defeat to Torquay United. Supplier of much of Bobby Zamora's ammunition with his pinpoint crosses, free-kicks and corners, Watto was a popular member of the side from 1999 until his free transfer to Woking in October 2005. Neville Southall, the then 40-year-old former Welsh international goalkeeper, kept Micky Adams's side at bay as the Devonians run out 1-0 winners at Withdean.

SATURDAY 22nd AUGUST 1959

The biggest-ever crowd for an opening game at the Goldstone – 31,828 – are in attendance for the visit of Aston Villa, newly-relegated from the top flight, in Division Two. The West Stand was under construction. Record £13,000 purchase Bill Curry made his debut in the 2-1 reverse. The striker arrived from Newcastle United and netted 26 times, including three hat-tricks, in his first season.

SATURDAY 22nd AUGUST 1964

Just six months earlier, Bobby Smith had been scoring for first division Tottenham Hotspur and England. On this day, the centre-forward made his debut for Brighton & Hove Albion in the fourth division! A Goldstone crowd of 20,058 were not disappointed – the striker bagged a brace as Archie Macaulay's swept aside visitors Barrow 3-1.

WEDNESDAY 22nd AUGUST 1979

Teddy Maybank scored Albion's first top-flight goal in the club's inaugural first division away fixture; a 2-1 defeat at Aston Villa.

SATURDAY 23rd AUGUST 1952

A 4-1 home win over Crystal Palace in the third division (south) was a great start to the 1952/53 campaign. Both debutants – Jimmy Leadbetter and Les Owens – scored in front of 23,905 Goldstone fans.

SATURDAY 23rd AUGUST 1959

After nearly 30 seasons – straddling two World Wars – Albion finally played their first game in the second division. Unfortunately, the trip to Middlesbrough coincided with a prolific Brian Clough firing on all cylinders. The striker scored five times in the 9-0 demolition.

SATURDAY 23rd AUGUST 1986

In the programme for the Portsmouth game, manager Alan Mullery declares: 'It's great to be back here at the Goldstone and, to be honest, the place hasn't changed that much in the last five years.' The game ends 0-0.

TUESDAY 23rd AUGUST 2005

Albion's tallest player to date, 6ft 6ins French keeper Florent Chaigneau, made his debut in the 3-2 League Cup defeat at Shrewsbury Town.

SATURDAY 24th AUGUST 1957

Albion chairman Major Carlo Campbell discussed the club's bonus structure after the 1-0 opening day win at Gillingham: "This first match has cost us a tidy sum in bonus money, but we don't mind paying this sort of cash." The amount was £4 per player on top of the maximum weekly wage of £17.

SATURDAY 24th AUGUST 1968

Six different goalscorers registered in the 6-0 third division (south) Goldstone thrashing of Oldham Athletic; Paul Flood, Stewart Henderson, Charlie Livesey, Howard Wilkinson, Kit Napier and John Templeman.

FRIDAY 24th AUGUST 1990

It was the day before the big kick-off to the 1990-91 campaign and manager Barry Lloyd was pulling out all the stops in the transfer market. Winger Clive Walker arrived for £20,000 from Fulham, Russel Bromage moved from Bristol City after 395 league appearances for the Ashton Gate outfit – and John Byrne made the short hop across the English Channel in a £125,000 deal from Le Havre.

SATURDAY 25th AUGUST 1945

Left-back Arthur Rowley made his wartime football debut in a 2-1 defeat at Reading. The Black Countryman netted once in five Albion starts and would join Fulham in 1948 where he moved to inside-forward. His goalscoring skills quickly became evident and he went on to notch an incredible 434 strikes in 619 league matches for the Cottagers, Leicester City and Shrewsbury Town.

WEDNESDAY 25th AUGUST 1948

A healthy crowd of 24,432 was in attendance at Ashton Gate to see Des Tennant make his Albion debut against Bristol City. The big Welshman could play anywhere down the right side and scored 23 of his 47 Albion goals – in 424 appearances – from the penalty spot during his 11 years at the club. An automatic choice, Des was presented with a writing bureau on completion of a decade's service and, after working as chief scout, became landlord of the Allen Arms in Lewes Road, Brighton.

SATURDAY 26th AUGUST 1922

The first player born outside the UK and Ireland to represent Albion, New Zealand-born George Moorhead made his one and only appearance in the 0-0 home draw with Norwich City.

SATURDAY 26th AUGUST 1939

The season kicked off with a goalless Goldstone draw against Port Vale. Football League competition was aborted after only two more games as Europe descended into war.

WEDNESDAY 26th AUGUST 1998

The battle for Withdean came to a close as SWEAT – the group of local residents opposed to the club's move – informed Brighton & Hove Council that they were withdrawing their application for a judicial review. Surely the Albion would be home soon now…

SATURDAY 27th AUGUST 1960

Bristol Rovers were thumped 6-1 in this Division Two fixture at the Goldstone. Local lad Adrian Thorne grabbed four while Freddie Jones and Bill Curry netted one apiece.

SATURDAY 27th AUGUST 1983

Albion returned back down to earth with a bump after their FA Cup Final exploits three months and six days earlier. Just 5,750 fans – a fraction of the Wembley crowd on that famous May day – were in attendance as Oldham Athletic won 1-0 at Boundary Park in the second division.

TUESDAY 27th AUGUST 1996

A 3-0 defeat at Barnet would perhaps be remembered for the birth of the most popular protest song: 'Build a Bonfire'. It was taken up for the first time on the Underhill terraces and became the title of a superb book on the troubled final years at the Goldstone Ground.

MONDAY 27th AUGUST 2001

It was a Bank Holiday special at Withdean. Fellow seasiders Blackpool were brushed aside as the Albion cantered to their 10th – including seven from last season – successive home victory, winning 4-0 with strikes from Charlie Oatway, Richard Carpenter, Lee Steele and Bobby Zamora.

SATURDAY 28th AUGUST 1920

Albion lost their first ever league game, 2-0 to Southend United at the Essex town's Kursaal Ground.

SATURDAY 28th AUGUST 1943

Polish airman Bishek Szajna-Stankowski made his solitary Albion appearance between the sticks in the 4-0 defeat at Reading.

SATURDAY 28th AUGUST 1979

Signed from Pompey for £150,000, defender Steve Foster made his first of two Albion debuts in the home League Cup second round first leg win over Cambridge United. The stopper became one of only three Albion players to gain senior England honours while on the books of the club, when he played in three matches in 1982, one of which was against Kuwait in the World Cup finals. A move to Aston Villa in 1984 was short-lived and Foster was sold to Luton Town, where he captained the Bedfordshire outfit in the 1988 League Cup triumph. One more transfer to Oxford and Fozzie was back home in Hove for three more seasons from 1992. Arguably one of the club's finest-ever players, the Portsmouth-born stopper netted 15 times in a total of 332 Albion appearances.

SATURDAY 29th AUGUST 1936

Inside-right Joe Wilson was in the Albion starting line-up for the first time in the 1-0 defeat at Gillingham. Born in County Durham, Joe scored 49 goals in 353 appearances for the club between 1936 and 1947, having joined from Newcastle United. He retired, aged 38, and began an 18-year stint as assistant trainer. Rarely seen without his trademark pipe, Joe's sprints to attend injured players became stuff of legend at the Goldstone. With brother Glen, the Wilsons devoted 68 years to the Albion: true club legends.

SATURDAY 29th AUGUST 1981

The 1-1 first division draw at West Ham United kicked off the third successive top-flight campaign. The game marked Mike Bailey's first game as manager following the 39-year-old's resignation from Charlton Athletic. The Boleyn Ground draw also saw the debuts of Jimmy Case, Don Shanks and Tony Grealish.

SATURDAY 30th AUGUST 1919

One of the most important men in the club's history, Charlie Webb began his managerial career with a 2-1 defeat at Brentford in the Southern League first division. The Irishman played three times for the Republic during a seven-year Goldstone playing spell that saw 79 goals in 275 appearances at inside-left. On demob after World War I in 1919, Charlie took on the immense task of re-building the Albion from the ground up in his role as manager. In the following 28 years, the great man built many a fine team on a shoestring budget.

SATURDAY 30th AUGUST 1969

The club's magnificent start to the campaign continued with a 2-1 win at Gigg Lane after strikes from Alan Gilliver and Kit Napier. The triumph at Bury was the Albion's fourth in the first five games and would be followed by two more consecutive victories.

MONDAY 30th AUGUST 1972

Former England international Barry Bridges was signed for a club record fee of £29,000 from Millwall by manager Pat Saward. The 31 year-old striker never quite reached the heights of his earlier career and only managed 14 goals in 71 appearances during a two-year stint on the south coast.

SATURDAY 31st AUGUST 1921

Northern Ireland international Jack Doran grabbed a hat-trick in the 3-0 third division (south) victory at Exeter City. The centre-forward scored the club's first 12 goals of the season!

SATURDAY 31st AUGUST 1935

Bert Stephens made the first of his 366 appearances in the 3-2 Goldstone win over Torquay United. The Gillingham-born outside-left netted on 174 occasions, 78 of which came during the war.

SATURDAY 31st AUGUST 1946

Local Sussex paper *The Evening Argus* reported that the Goldstone Ground, Albion's headquarters should now be known as 'HMS Goldstone' – because "so resplendent are the stands and fencing painted in battleship grey".

Brighton & Hove Albion

ON THIS DAY

SEPTEMBER

THURSDAY 1st SEPTEMBER 1898

Albion forefathers Brighton United won their first-ever game, 8-1, away against Southwick. The friendly fixture kicked off at 6pm.

SATURDAY 1st SEPTEMBER 1979

Albion enjoyed their first ever win in Division One. Peter Ward, Paul Clark and Brian Horton were all on target as Bolton Wanderers are dispatched 3-1 at the Goldstone Ground. The programme features penpal requests from an Ipswich Town fan and an 18-year-old locksmith who supports VfB Nufringen in Germany.

WEDNESDAY 2nd SEPTEMBER 1908

Right-half Billy Booth made his debut in the Albion's 3-1 home defeat to Southampton. The Sheffield-born defender was part of the successful side that won the Southern League Championship, FA Charity Shield and the Southern Charity Cup in the club's early golden age. Despite a career interrupted by World War I, Billy managed 12 goals in 369 appearances before leaving for his native Yorkshire as Albion became founder members of the third division (south) in 1920. Also against the Saints that day, Joe Leeming made the first of his 238 starts for the club. The Lancashire-born full-back didn't find the net once! Another eight players appeared for the first time.

SATURDAY 2nd SEPTEMBER 1978

A fantastic weekend for Sussex Sport: Albion won 4-1 at Millwall; Sussex beat Somerset to win the Gillette Cup, Steve Ovett collected a gold medal at the European Athletics Championships in Prague and Eastbourne speedway rider Gordon Kennett finished runner-up in the World Final at Wembley. The following day a Peter Graves XI – which included Norman Wisdom – took on an Albion XI at the County Ground; the footballers won!

TUESDAY 2nd SEPTEMBER 1997

One of the biggest results in the Albion's history came off the pitch as the despised regime of Bill Archer, Greg Stanley and David Bellotti are finally replaced by new owners: the consortium included Dick Knight, Bob Pinnock and Martin Perry after two years of bitter fighting. Things were looking up…

SATURDAY 3rd SEPTEMBER 1904

The 2-2 draw at New Brompton (now Gillingham) was notable for the change of shirt: replacing all blue, Albion wore blue and white stripes for the very first time. Eight players made their debuts: Mark Mellors, Tim Robertson, Paddy Gilhooly, Archie Livingstone, Joe O'Brien, Andy Gardner, Mickey Good, Ben Hulse and Tommy Aspden.

SATURDAY 3rd SEPTEMBER 1927

In the third match of the season at Luton Town, Albion enjoyed their second 5-2 victory. Tommy Cook, Tommy Simpson, defender Paul Mooney (2) and Jimmy Hopkins scored in front of 9,468 fans.

SATURDAY 3rd SEPTEMBER 1932

George Ansell, Bobby Farrell (2) and Arthur Attwood found the net in a 4-0 victory at Watford. Just three days earlier Albion had lost 5-0 at Selhurst Park!

WEDNESDAY 3rd SEPTEMBER 1958

A crowd of 39,520 were at Anfield for Albion's first ever competitive game under floodlights. Liverpool won 5-0 in the second division fixture.

SATURDAY 3rd SEPTEMBER 1960

Albion lost their third successive game on the road in the 2-0 second division defeat at Liverpool. The crowd of 24,390 was over 15,000 down on the corresponding fixture exactly two years earlier.

SATURDAY 3rd SEPTEMBER 1983

Chelsea fans in the 20,874 crowd celebrated their 2-1 second division victory by snapping the North Stand crossbar at the Goldstone.

WEDNESDAY 3rd SEPTEMBER 1997

Albion's new era under Dick Knight began with a 2-2 draw against Peterborough United at Gillingham in front of just 1,215 diehard fans.

TUESDAY 3rd SEPTEMBER 2002

Fatboy Slim, aka Norman Cook, forked out £500,000 to become one of Brighton and Hove Albion's leading shareholders, giving him an 11 per cent stake in the club's holding company.

SATURDAY 4th SEPTEMBER 1920

Around 11,000 fans were at the Goldstone Ground for this third division (south) contest with Southend United. In the newly-formed division, clubs played each other home and away on consecutive weeks. Jack Doran's solitary strike – the club's first goal scored in the Football League – avenged a 2-0 defeat at Southend United the previous week.

MONDAY 4th SEPTEMBER 1950

Described as a 'chunky little player' in Tim Carder and Roger Harris's excellent Albion A-Z, A Who's Who, Frankie Howard made his debut for the club in the 1-1 third division (south) draw at Millwall. The outside-left – who was rejected for National Service because of his flat feet – was one of the quickest players to wear the stripes and notched 31 goals in 219 appearances. He became groundsman in 1962 – after ligament injury prematurely ended his career aged 28 – and tended to the highly-regarded Goldstone turf for 31 years until a cold-hearted David Bellotti savagely made the stalwart redundant in a cost-cutting exercise in 1993.

SATURDAY 4th SEPTEMBER 1976

Goals from Tony Towner, Ian Mellor and Fred Binney earned the points in a 3-1 win over Rotherham United at the Goldstone. It was the first time under new manager Alan Mullery that Albion had topped the third division table.

WEDNESDAY 4th SEPTEMBER 1991

A very strange night at The Den began as Perry Digweed injured himself during the warm-up. His replacement, defender Gary Chivers, performed admirably between the sticks for eight minutes until Mark Beeney, who had been sitting in the stand expecting to watch the game was changed and ready to enter the fray. John Byrne and Robert Codner scored the goals in a 2-1 victory over Millwall but the contest is also remembered for a bizarre pitch invasion... by a 14-year-old! The youngster vaulted the fence from the stand alongside the pitch and karate-kicked John Robinson in the back before being wrestled to the ground by Beeney and led away by police officers.

MONDAY 5th SEPTEMBER 1910

The Albion were crowned 'Champions of All England.' Before Premiership winners faced that season's FA Cup winners in the traditional football season curtain-raiser, the Southern League champions would face the Football League title winners for the Charity Shield. The season had already kicked off when Aston Villa – league champions six times in the previous 16 years – faced Albion at Stamford Bridge. In the 72nd minute Bill Hastings threaded a pass through to Charlie Webb who jinked past two Villa defenders before powering home a rising cross shot. The Midlanders didn't win the league again for another 70 years.

SATURDAY 5th SEPTEMBER 1959

A Bill Curry hat-trick secured a 3-1 second division victory over Portsmouth at the Goldstone. Historically, 5th September is a good day for the Albion. The club have won 12 of their 21 league fixtures on this day, but three of the defeats have been heavy: 1-5 at Millwall (1949), 0-5 at Ipswich Town (1951) and 0-4 at Bristol Rovers (1972).

MONDAY 5th SEPTEMBER 1987

Barry Lloyd's summer transfers are listed in the programme as: thirteen incoming players at £357,000 and four outgoing – Terry Connor, Danny Wilson, Dean Saunders and Eric Young – for a total of £470,000.

FRIDAY 6th SEPTEMBER 1901

The Argus announced Albion's election into the Southern League second division. 'It is hoped that football enthusiasts will turn up in large numbers, and to show the executive that their efforts to improve the class of football in the district are appreciated.'

TUESDAY 6th SEPTEMBER 1977

The Goldstone hosted an England Under-21 game against Norway. Peter Ward scored a hat-trick in a 6-0 win on his international debut!

THURSDAY 6th SEPTEMBER 2007

After years of marches, letter-writing, protests, sit-ins, lock-outs, flower-sending, political party-forming, leaflet-dropping, postcard-distributing and petition-signing, Albion fans could finally, without the threat of appeal, celebrate planning permission for the new stadium at Falmer.

Saturday 7th September 1901

On a training pitch on Dyke Road Albion played their first ever fixture. The club were due to host Shoreham at Sussex CCC's County Ground in Eaton Road, Hove, but the fixture clashed with a cricket match. Albion, who played in 'fisherman's blue' shirts and white 'knickers', won 2-0 in front of a 'fair attendance' with Clem Barker notching the club's first-ever goal. Over the other side of town, the Hove Football Club launched their new venture – 'the well-appointed private ground which they named the Goldstone Ground' – with a 3-0 friendly defeat to Clapton.

Saturday 7th September 1907

Duncan Ronaldson and Jimmy Burnett made goalscoring debuts in the 3-1 Goldstone victory over Queens Park Rangers. Tom Morris, Dick Wombwell and Arthur Archer also enjoyed their first Albion run-outs.

Saturday 7th September 1929

Dan Kirkwood scored four in the 6-3 Goldstone third division (south) win over Norwich City. The gate was 7,546.

Saturday 7th September 1957

Peter Harburn scored the only goal at Queens Park Rangers. Albion's third successive victory on the road was marred when home fans tried to storm the dressing-room through the players' tunnel. One fan got into the referee's room.

Wednesday 7th September 1966

In the programme versus Bournemouth, the Post Bag section dealt with two issues: a fan asked why supporters don't use 'the Shrimps' as a nickname to which the club replies: 'Albion is the word we use – short, easy and it just suits us'; several letters arrive at the Goldstone Ground concerning the 'use of horns, rattles, bells, whistles and trumpets during the Swindon match'. The club reply: 'Noise is all part of the soccer scene, but we feel certain our followers will co-operate in not making an unnecessary disturbance'.

Tuesday 7th September 1982

Albion registered their first Division One victory of the campaign. Gerry Ryan scored in the 1-0 Goldstone triumph over Arsenal.

SATURDAY 8th SEPTEMBER 1984

Frank Worthington, Terry Connor, Steve Penney and Gary Howlett hit the target during a 4-2 Division Two win at Cardiff City.

MONDAY 8th SEPTEMBER 1997

Ian Baird scored his last Albion goal in the rearranged game at Colchester United, moved due to Princess Diana's funeral. The 3-1 loss left the Seagulls 22nd in the third division.

SATURDAY 8th SEPTEMBER 2006

Former first-team coach Dean Wilkins took charge of his first game after Mark McGhee's dismissal, at Millwall's New Den. Despite Richard Carpenter's first-half dismissal, 10-man Albion battled bravely and earned the three points when Dean Cox's 88th-minute free-kick deflected in off Marvin Elliott.

WEDNESDAY 9th SEPTEMBER 1970

Kurt Nogan was born in Cardiff. The striker arrived on a free transfer from Luton Town in 1992 and became the first player to score more than 20 goals in consecutive seasons since Albert Mundy (1954 to 1957). He moved to Burnley for £250,000 in February 1995, having scored 60 times in 120 Albion run-outs.

SATURDAY 9th SEPTEMBER 1972

Albion moved up to 15th place with their first second division win for a decade: a 2-1 home win over Fulham. John Templeman's goal and a penalty from Bert Murray secured the points after five games without a win.

WEDNESDAY 9th SEPTEMBER 1981

Rotterdam, Holland, was the setting for Michael Robinson's second international goal, for the Republic of Ireland against the Dutch.

SATURDAY 9th SEPTEMBER 1989

A quite extraordinary second division match at Bramall Lane. Albion went three down to Sheffield United – only to come back, through two goals each from Kevin Bremner and Paul Wood to lead 4-3! The Blades sharpened up their act and ran out 5-4 eventual winners. Three days later, Albion scored four on the road again at Wolves.

WEDNESDAY 10th SEPTEMBER 1980

Dublin was the venue for Ireland's World Cup qualifier against the Netherlands. Mark Lawrenson scores his second goal for the Republic during the 2-1 win.

SATURDAY 10th SEPTEMBER 1989

In the middle of an eight-game losing run, Albion faced Bournemouth at the Goldstone for this second division fixture. Goalkeeper Perry Digweed was caught in traffic and failed to make kick-off so John Keeley, despite failing a morning fitness test, deputised. The former taxi driver – with injured fingers strapped – couldn't stop the Cherries winning 2-1.

SATURDAY 11th SEPTEMBER 1948

Albion lost 6-2 at Millwall in a third division (south) fixture to end a six-match unbeaten start to the campaign.

SATURDAY 11th SEPTEMBER 1981

Albion led the way in promoting recycling. Glass bottle-banks appeared across Brighton carrying a club advert.

TUESDAY 11th SEPTEMBER 2001

The Twin Towers disaster in New York dominated everyone's thoughts at Withdean. In an understandably muted atmosphere, Albion lost 3-0 to Southampton in the Worthington Cup second round.

SATURDAY 12th SEPTEMBER 1981

Steve Gatting made his debut in the 1-0 first division defeat at Everton. Born in Middlesex, the defender's brother Mike captained England at cricket, and his son Joe also played for the club. Left-footer Steve played in the FA Cup Final, at right-back in the replay, and was an ever-present as Albion won promotion in 1988. Steve made 369 appearances, scoring 21 times.

TUESDAY 12th SEPTEMBER 1989

Albion maintained a 100% record over Wolverhampton Wanderers by beating them for the ninth successive time in Football League meetings between the club. Garry Nelson, Kevin Bremner (2) and Robert Codner scored at Molineux in a 4-2 Division Two victory.

SATURDAY 13th SEPTEMBER 1902

Ben Garfield made his debut in the 4-2 Southern League Division Two victory over Southall. His signing was a major coup for the fledgling club; the outside-left had played for England just four years earlier. The winger had netted 38 goals in 117 appearances for West Bromwich Albion before his shock move south. He went on to bang in 29 in 64 starts for Brighton.

SATURDAY 13th SEPTEMBER 1975

Albion began a club record run of 14 consecutive home victories with a 6-0 thrashing of Chester City. The crowd of 7,924 saw goals from Fred Binney (2), Peter O'Sullivan, Ian Mellor and Gerry Fell (2) to get the club back to winning Goldstone ways after two straight defeats.

SATURDAY 13th SEPTEMBER 1997

Darlington fan Paul Heeny became new Albion fanzine Scars and Stripes' first ever customer at Priestfield. The 28-page publication worked tirelessly during the two-year period in Kent and raised nearly £10,000 before the final edition in early 2000.

WEDNESDAY 14th SEPTEMBER 1949

Fred Leamon made his debut in the third division (south) 3-0 defeat at Reading. The centre-forward netted four times in 11 Albion starts, but died of a heart attack while working as a security guard at the wedding of Prince Charles and Lady Diana Spencer in 1981.

SATURDAY 15th SEPTEMBER 1956

Albion thrashed Torquay United 6-0 in front of 15,856 fans at the Goldstone Ground.

SATURDAY 15th SEPTEMBER 1979

Gary Stevens made his full Albion debut as a 17-year-old in a first division game at the Goldstone versus Ipswich Town. The accomplished defender scored the equaliser in the FA Cup Final and went on to score three times in 152 appearances. Sold to Tottenham Hotspur as a 21-year-old for £300,000 in 1983, Gary won the UEFA Cup in his first season and represented England seven times.

TUESDAY 16th SEPTEMBER 1969

With a scoreline of 1-1 at Orient, the referee abandoned the match due a muddy pitch and worsening weather conditions. The 5,518 spectators were not happy and the officials had to be escorted from the pitch by the Metropolitan Police.

THURSDAY 16th SEPTEMBER 1982

Pint-sized Leon Knight was born in Hackney, London. The striker scored 34 times in 108 Albion appearances.

SATURDAY 16th SEPTEMBER 1989

Barry Lloyd's side beat West Ham United 3-0 at the Goldstone with first-half efforts from Kevin Bremner, Robert Codner and Garry Nelson. The win moved Albion up to second in Division Two.

SATURDAY 17th SEPTEMBER 1983

Local press report that an Anglo-American syndicate were to join the board. The club denied all knowledge and assured fans that the current board will 'continue to work for the good of Brighton & Hove Albion, the supporters come first'. Also in the programme for the 1-1 draw versus Carlisle United, Gordon Smith recalled the time he went to Paul McCartney's house and had the privilege of a private gig by the ex-Beatle.

SATURDAY 18th SEPTEMBER 1926

The most goals in an Albion Football League match is 12; a 9-3 home win over Swindon Town. Sam Jennings scored four times, England forward Tommy Cook netted twice while Andy Neil, Jack Nightingale and Wally Little (pen) grabbed one each.

SUNDAY 18th SEPTEMBER 1938

Charlie Livesey was born in London. The clever forward scored 37 times in 146 appearances between 1965 and 1969.

SATURDAY 18th SEPTEMBER 1976

Fred Binney made his last Albion appearance. In a game featured on Match of the Day, 15,605 fans watch Peter Ward (2), Steve Piper, Peter O'Sullivan, Ian Mellor (2) and Gerry Fell hit the target in the 7-2 Division Three walloping of York City.

SATURDAY 19th SEPTEMBER 1925

A brace from Wally Little and a single strike from Tommy Cook earned the points in a 3-2 Division Three (South) victory over Crystal Palace at the Goldstone.

WEDNESDAY 19th SEPTEMBER 1990

South coast rivals Portsmouth were the visitors for this Division Two clash. Mike Small, Robert Codner and Dean Wilkins scored the goals in the 3-1 win to move the Seagulls up to sixth place.

SATURDAY 20th SEPTEMBER 1919

Bandy-legged Wally Little makes his first Albion start in the 3-1 Goldstone Southern League Division One victory over Bristol Rovers. The Middlesex man switched from left-back to left-half, becoming a crowd favourite, and holds the record for penalties scored; 26 of his 36 Albion goals in 332 appearances came from the spot.

SATURDAY 20th SEPTEMBER 1952

Eric Gill let in a goal on his Albion debut in the 3-1 win over Leyton Orient at the Goldstone. The 5ft 10ins keeper had no chance as Sam Bartram's understudy at Charlton Athletic so Billy Lane paid £400 for his services in June 1952.

MONDAY 20th SEPTEMBER 2004

Brian Clough died of stomach cancer aged 69. Best remembered for winning successive European Cups with Nottingham Forest in 1979 and 1980, the outspoken manager famously joined Albion after taking Derby County to their first league championship in 1971/72. Clough spent only eight months at Albion before leaving for Leeds United in July 1974.

SATURDAY 21st SEPTEMBER 1901

Albion played their first-ever competitive game; a preliminary FA Cup 6-2 win over Brighton Athletic at the Sussex County Cricket Ground.

WEDNESDAY 21st SEPTEMBER 1994

Liam Brady's men beat Premiership Leicester City 1-0 in a League Cup second round tie at the Goldstone. Kurt Nogan's strike was watched by an 11,481 crowd.

THURSDAY 22nd SEPTEMBER 1910

Fans gathered at The Dome for a 'smoking concert' to celebrate the Albion's FA Charity Shield triumph.

SATURDAY 22nd SEPTEMBER 1928

Bobby Farrell made his Albion debut in the 3-1 third division (south) defeat at Norwich City. The diminutive Scot joined after a failed trial along the coast at Portsmouth and was a huge favourite at the Goldstone. A great character, the outside-right netted 95 goals in 466 appearances for the club.

SUNDAY 22nd SEPTEMBER 1996

Protestors demonstrated outside the Liberal Democrat Conference at the Brighton Centre holding a banner which read 'If one Lib-Dem [David Bellotti] can ruin a football club, think what a Lib-Dem government could do to the country'.

SATURDAY 23rd SEPTEMBER 1922

Albion legend Tommy Cook made his debut in the Division Three (South) 0-0 draw at Queens Park Rangers.

SATURDAY 23rd SEPTEMBER 1967

Albion had not won an away game in the league for eight months; not the best preparation for Nobby Lawton's debut! The midfielder was a Busby Babe but couldn't establish himself under Sir Matt and was transferred to Preston North End for £20,000 in 1963. After captaining North End in the FA Cup Final a year later, the Mancunian was snapped up by Archie Macaulay in 1967. His experience made the difference in a 2-1 win at Orient – Brian Tawse and Kit Napier were the goalscorers.

TUESDAY 23rd SEPTEMBER 1975

Albion moved up to seventh after Barry Butlin scored the only goal in a 1-0 third division win at Crystal Palace.

WEDNESDAY 23rd SEPTEMBER 1992

David Beckham made his competitive debut for Manchester United coming on as substitute at the Goldstone. Matthew Edwards scored Albion's goal in the 1-1 League Cup draw in front of a 16,649 crowd.

SATURDAY 24th SEPTEMBER 1949

Bournemouth and Boscombe Athletic's Dean Court was the venue for Glen Wilson's Albion debut. The County Durham-born left-half joined the club after being spotted by player-coach Jack Dugnolle playing for Fareham Town against Albion's 'A' team. The defender, who began his career at Newcastle United, once featured in a league XI that beat the Dutch national side 6-1 in 1956! Glen – who made 436 appearances, netting 28 times – was a member of the backroom staff for nearly 20 years until his untimely departure as part of an economy drive in 1986.

WEDNESDAY 24th SEPTEMBER 1969

A massive crowd of 32,539 packed into the Goldstone for a League Cup third round tie with Wolverhampton Wanderers. Alan Gilliver and Eddie Spearitt registered in the 3-2 reverse.

SUNDAY 25th SEPTEMBER 1938

Wally Gould was born in Yorkshire. As a 23-year-old, the winger joined from York City for £4,000 in 1964 and played a vital role in Albion's fourth division championship success a year later, top-scoring with 21 goals and missing only three games. A fixture for four seasons, Wally was reluctantly released to enjoy a successful spell in South Africa.

THURSDAY 25th SEPTEMBER 1952

Ray Clarke was born in Hackney, London. He made his name at Mansfield Town, scoring 28 goals as they won the fourth division in 1975. Another prolific season prompted a move Sparta Rotterdam and then on to Ajax where he scored 38 times as they won a league-and-cup double in 1978/79. Alan Mullery paid £175,000 for Clarke, and he played a part – 9 strikes in 33 appearances – in retaining first division status in 1980. He moved to Newcastle United before injury forced retirement.

SATURDAY 25TH SEPTEMBER 1999

Paul Rogers' last-minute strike earned Albion a 1-0 win against Cheltenham Town, the club's seventh consecutive victory on this date.

THURSDAY 25th SEPTEMBER 2003

Former Albion manager Peter Taylor snubbed an approach from Reading to take over at the Madejski Stadium, in favour of Hull City.

SATURDAY 26TH SEPTEMBER 1903

Albion enjoyed their first-ever win at Fratton Park. George Rushton, Ben Garfield and an own-goal earned a 3-0 Southern League first division victory over Portsmouth.

TUESDAY 26th SEPTEMBER 1995

On-loan Gary Bull scored twice in the 4-1 win at Cambridge United – in the Auto Windscreens Shield. The game also marked the debut of former England international Russell Osman. After 18 months without first-team action, the defender couldn't live up to his distinguished reputation during his 11 run-outs on the south coast.

MONDAY 26th SEPTEMBER 2005

At least 10,000 fans – including Des Lynam, Norman Cook, local celebrities plus countless ex-players and current squad members – marched on the Labour Party Conference at the Brighton Centre. The procession started from Madeira Drive and snaked along the seafront as the vociferous throng showed their support for a new stadium at Falmer, hoping that Deputy Prime Minister John Prescott would take notice of the huge groundswell of support from the people of Sussex.

SATURDAY 27th SEPTEMBER 1980

Brian Horton netted a penalty in the 4-1 defeat to league champions Liverpool at Anfield.

SATURDAY 27th SEPTEMBER 1997

Defenders Mark Morris and Stuart Tuck both found the target for the first 'home' victory for Albion during their time ground-sharing with Gillingham. The 2-1 win over Rochdale moved the Seagulls up to 22nd in the basement division.

MONDAY 27th SEPTEMBER 2004

Over 5,000 Albion fans – complete with whistles, drums, hundreds of banners, placards and very loud voices – converged on the Labour Conference at the Brighton Centre to urge the Government to say yes to the club's new stadium at Falmer. Brighton Pavilion Labour MP David Lepper said: "We have got to look no further than Falmer. It is the best site. This march shows the support for it."

SATURDAY 28th SEPTEMBER 1935

Albion's indifferent start to the third division (south) season ended. After a 5-0 loss at Coventry City a week earlier, vengeance was wreaked on Newport County with a 7-1 mauling at the Goldstone Ground!

WEDNESDAY 28TH SEPTEMBER 1955

Hot on the heels of a 5-0 demolition of Southampton at the Goldstone Ground, Ipswich Town are the Hove visitors. Nearly 14,000 fans see an Albert Mundy brace and a Peter Harburn strike earn a 3-0 victory.

THURSDAY 28th SEPTEMBER 1972

Devout Christian Stuart Munday was born in West Ham, London. The right-back scored five excellent goals in his 117 appearances – including an absolute screamer at Leicester City in the 1994/95 League Cup.

SATURDAY 29th SEPTEMBER 1900

Shirebrook, Derbyshire is the birthplace of Albert Sykes. The former coal miner made 16 starts for the Albion between 1926 and 1928 after moving from Notts County.

WEDNESDAY 29th SEPTEMBER 1926

Albion finally purchased the Goldstone Ground on a 99-year lease from the Stanford Estate, after originally sub-letting from Alderman Clark.

SATURDAY 29th SEPTEMBER 1962

'Mr Reliable' Norman Gall makes his Albion debut in the 2-0 third division defeat at Watford's Vicarage Road – a day before his 20th birthday. Born in Wallsend, the defender was signed from Gateshead where he played as an amateur. Winning 'Player of the Season' twice – in 1971 and 1974 – Norman went on to play 488 times for the Albion, netting four goals.

SATURDAY 29th SEPTEMBER 1979

Albion drew 2-2 with the other Albion, West Bromwich, at the Hawthorns. The programme explains that 'Argentinean wonderboy Diego Maradona was prevented from his country's European tour because of army duties'.

WEDNESDAY 30th SEPTEMBER 1936

The wartime years' greatest stalwart, Stan Risdon, pulled on an Albion shirt for the first time. Having made only 21 league starts at the outbreak of World War II, the utility man from Exeter started an incredible run of appearing in 216 of the 243 wartime fixtures. On the re-introduction of league football in 1946, Stan was 33 and featured on just three more occasions.

SATURDAY 30th SEPTEMBER 1972

Richard Carpenter was born in Sheppey, Kent. The midfielder achieved promotion with Gillingham, Fulham and Cardiff City before winning two divisional titles and a play-off final after joining the Seagulls in 2000. The antiques collector made 252 appearances, scoring 20 times for Albion. He is fondly remembered for his committed displays and wonderful goals.

SATURDAY 30th SEPTEMBER 1978

Two own-goals by the same player – Mick Baxter – helped Albion to a 5-1 victory over Preston North End at the Goldstone. Gerry Ryan, Peter Ward and Paul Clark notched a strike apiece in front of 19,217 fans to move the Seagulls up to third place in the second division.

Brighton & Hove Albion

ON THIS DAY

OCTOBER

SATURDAY 1st OCTOBER 1932

Secretary Albert Underwood famously forgot to register Albion for exemption from the four qualifying rounds of the FA Cup! As a result, Sussex County League Shoreham visited the Goldstone and were promptly hammered 12-0! Arthur Attwood hit a double hat-trick.

SATURDAY 1st OCTOBER 1966

Kit Napier's Albion career was off to a flier! The forward grabbed a brace in the 5-2 home victory over Peterborough United. Signed by Archie Macaulay for £8,500 from Newcastle United, the two-footed striker scored 10 or more goals in each of his six seasons; the only Albion player to do so in peacetime. After a fall-out with manager Pat Saward, the popular player moved to third division Blackburn Rovers for £15,000. His 99 goals in 291 appearances was bettered only by Tommy Cook.

THURSDAY 1st OCTOBER 1981

Goalkeeper David Yelldell was born in Stuttgart, Germany. The big stopper started in three games during 2004/05 and, as 2007/08 started, was playing American football for the Stuttgart Kickers.

SATURDAY 1st OCTOBER 1983

The 11,517 fans present at the Goldstone couldn't believe their eyes; Albion were leading previously unbeaten Charlton Athletic 5-0 at half-time! The incredible final score of 7-0 included a Jimmy Case hat-trick, a Gerry Ryan brace and one apiece from Gordon Smith and Terry Connor. Despite the magnificent result, rumours abound that coach Chris Cattlin was picking the team.

TUESDAY 1st OCTOBER 1996

Before the home fixture with Lincoln City, chairman Bill Archer completely rejected the proposed consortium takeover, much to the chagrin of the 4,411 Goldstone spectators. When the Imps opened the scoring in the 25th minute, a pitch invasion by desperate fans resulted in the players leaving the pitch, holding the game up for 13 minutes. The suspended points deduction imposed following the abandonment of the York City game the previous April would now be imposed. The 3-1 defeat left Jimmy Case's men in second-to-last spot in the third division.

SATURDAY 2nd OCTOBER 1976

A bumper Goldstone crowd of 27,054 were in attendance for the third division visit of Crystal Palace. The 1-1 draw saw the home side overtaken at the summit by Shrewsbury Town.

MONDAY 2nd OCTOBER 2000

Micky Adams was awarded 'Manager of the Month' for September following a great run of 16 points from six games – including four straight wins without conceding a goal – which had lifted his team from 20th place to fourth in the third division.

SATURDAY 3rd OCTOBER 1959

Eastville, home of Bristol Rovers, was the setting for a remarkable match. The score was 2-2 at half-time; the second period saw the lead yo-yo between the sides before Albion eventually ran out 5-4 winners!

WEDNESDAY 3rd OCTOBER 1990

The club revealed that Harry Enfield's 'Loadsamoney' character filmed a sketch for his new TV comedy programme behind the North goal with groundsman Frankie Howard as an extra!

TUESDAY 4th OCTOBER 1955

Dublin was the birthplace of an Albion favourite. From a Gaelic football background, Gerry Ryan found himself at Derby County in September 1977. Virtually 365 days later, Alan Mullery brought the 22-year-old to the Goldstone in a £80,000 deal. Able to play on the wing, midfield or up front, Gerry was invaluable. His career – 39 goals in 199 run-outs – was cruelly ended, at the age of 29, courtesy of a scything 'tackle' by Crystal Palace's Henry Hughton in 1985.

TUESDAY 4th OCTOBER 2005

Probably the most amazing headline ever connected with Brighton & Hove Albion Football Club was printed in *The Argus*: 'Maradona Eyes Up Albion'. It was reported that the Argentinian – probably the best footballer of his generation – was eyeing up a takeover bid with his compatriot Ossie Ardiles. Chairman Dick Knight said of the revelation: "I believe it is distinctly probable that all sorts of people would be interested in the Albion when we get our stadium."

SATURDAY 5th OCTOBER 1957

Albion's new inside-forward Dave Sexton – who would later manage Chelsea, QPR and Manchester United – scored twice in his second appearance in a 5-3 home win over Newport County, which took the club back to the top of the third division (south) after four defeats.

TUESDAY 5th OCTOBER 1976

Alan Mullery, referring to a 7-0 third division Goldstone thumping of Walsall on this day, said: "The fans watched a terrible first half, which was like a practice match. We got to their 18-yard line and gave the ball away and they did likewise at the other end. At half-time the team were about to have some tea, but I threw all the tea cups up the wall and sent the players out into the centre circle to stand in the snow and rain and feel what the fans were feeling. Within 25 minutes they'd scored seven goals, with Peter Ward getting four and Ian Mellor three."

SATURDAY 5th OCTOBER 1985

Six different players scored in Albion's 6-1 second division demolition of Carlisle United: Mike Ferguson, Alan Biley, Danny Wilson, Steve Jacobs, Dean Saunders and Dennis Mortimer. Chris Cattlin's side remained fourth.

THURSDAY 6th OCTOBER 1927

John Ferrier was born in Edinburgh. The centre-forward made his only Albion appearance – albeit a goalscoring one – after team-mate Frank Hindley's train was stranded on the way to Torquay in the 1946/47 season.

SATURDAY 6th OCTOBER 1979

Not a great first league encounter with Manchester United in front of 52,641 at Old Trafford. Left-back Gary Williams and goalkeeper Eric Steele embarrassingly threw punches at each other in front of the Stretford End during the 2-0 first division reverse. Steele was placed on the transfer list soon after.

SATURDAY 6th OCTOBER 1984

Mick Ferguson – who scored seven goals in 21 games – made his Albion debut in the 2-0 second division home win over Birmingham City.

TUESDAY 7th OCTOBER 1911

Around 4,000 fans watched Albion thump Southampton 5-0 at the Goldstone in this Southern League fixture. Archie Needham (2), Billy Booth and Charlie Webb (2) were the goalscorers.

SATURDAY 7th OCTOBER 1978

The largest crowd ever to see an Albion/Palace clash – 33,685 – watched on at Selhurst Park as the Eagles continued their unbeaten run against the Seagulls with a 3-1 win. Brian Horton scored the consolation for Alan Mullery's side. It was eight games since an Albion victory over their rivals.

TUESDAY 7th OCTOBER 1980

Peter Ward scored in a 3-1 home defeat to Everton. It was the Liverpool club's 3,000th game in the first division.

SATURDAY 8th OCTOBER 1938

Stan Hurst scored both the goals in Albion's third division (south) victory over Ipswich Town at the Goldstone Ground. It was the Suffolk side's first season in the Football League.

SATURDAY 8th OCTOBER 1960

Ian McNeill and Roy Jennings hit the target as Albion drew 2-2 at Norwich City in front of 22,919 fans at Carrow Road.

SATURDAY 8th OCTOBER 1985

Bradford returned to their city – for the first time following the tragic fire at Valley Parade – to host Albion in a Milk Cup tie at the Odsal Stadium, home of rugby league outfit Bradford Northern. Chris Cattlin's men won 2-0.

TUESDAY 8th OCTOBER 2002

Martin Hinshelwood is moved upstairs into the role of director of football, after 11 straight Division One defeats, after Albion appointed Steve Coppell as manager. "Steve will bring a level of experience we feel is vital at this time. I have made him fully aware that no increase in the playing budget will suddenly be made available, but he understands the club's position – he is now eager to get started," proclaimed chairman Dick Knight.

FRIDAY 9th OCTOBER 1885

Albion legend Bert Longstaff was born in Shoreham-by-Sea. He made 443 appearances for Albion between 1906 and 1922.

SATURDAY 9th OCTOBER 1993

An injury crisis necessitated Albion boss Barry Lloyd fielding the club's youngest line-up in their history for a 1-1 draw with Stockport County at the Goldstone Ground. The average age of the team was a mere 21 years and 153 days and the team (with ages) was: Nicky Rust (19), Stuart Myall (18), Stuart Tuck (19), Ian Chapman (23), Stuart Munday (21), Paul McCarthy (22), Danny Simmonds (18), Simon Funnell (19), Kurt Nogan (23), Robert Codner (28) and Matthew Edwards (22). Kurt Nogan scored the Albion goal.

FRIDAY 9th OCTOBER 1998

The day after becoming the club second 'People's Player', Rod Thomas scored just 22 minutes into his Albion debut in the 3-2 win at Cambridge United. The winger joined from Chester City in a £25,000 deal and most of the fee was raised by the fans.

SATURDAY 10th OCTOBER 1964

Witnessed by a 14,261 gate, Albion enjoyed a third home win in seven days. Wally Gould, Jimmy Collins (2), Jack Smith (2), and Bobby Smith scored in the 6-0 drubbing of Notts County. The fixture also saw the debut of former Welsh international full-back Mel Hopkins.

WEDNESDAY 10th OCTOBER 2001

Bob Booker and Martin Hinshelwood were installed as caretaker managers following Micky Adams' resignation after two-and-a-half years in charge.

FRIDAY 10th OCTOBER 2003

Bizarrely, Bob Booker became caretaker manager (again) exactly two years after his first spell in the role. Previously he had kept the manager's hotseat warm prior to Peter Taylor's arrival. This time he stepped into the temporary position after Steve Coppell left Withdean for Reading.

SATURDAY 11th OCTOBER 1986

Goalkeeper John Keeley made his debut in the 1-0 defeat at Ipswich Town. The Essex-born stopper arrived for just £1,500 from Chelmsford City and was sold to Oldham Athletic – after 160 starts – for £240,000 in 1990.

SATURDAY 11th OCTOBER 1997

Captain Ian Baird was sent off at Chester City for two elbowing offences. Albion went down 2-0, leaving the club in 21st place in Division Three.

SATURDAY 12th OCTOBER 1957

Albion triumphed in a third division (south) fixture at Fellows Park, Walsall. Albert Mundy, Peter Harburn and Denis Foreman scored the goals to earn a 3-2 win that kept their side top.

WEDNESDAY 12th OCTOBER 1983

Despite Albion's relegation from the top flight, Tony Grealish was still good enough to represent his country in a European Championship qualifier. The midfielder couldn't do anything to stop a 3-2 Netherlands victory in Dublin.

TUESDAY 12th OCTOBER 1999

Defender Danny Cullip signed from Brentford for £50,000, after impressing during a four-match loan spell for the club. The inspirational defender led from the back in his five years on the coast and was a firm favourite with the Withdean faithful. After helping Albion win back-to-back league titles in 2001 and 2002, and win promotion in 2004 via the play-off final, fans were disappointed to see Cullip, by then the club captain, move to Sheffield United in 2004 for £250,000. He left with a record of 239 appearances and 10 goals.

MONDAY 13th OCTOBER 2003

Jake Robinson became Albion's youngest ever goalscorer, aged 16 and 355 days, when he slotted home a pass from Nathan Jones in the 88th minute against Forest Green Rovers in the second round of the LDV Vans Trophy.

SATURDAY 14th OCTOBER 1933

Len Darling made the first of 341 appearances in an Albion shirt in the 1-0 win at Aldershot. He played 113 matches during World War II.

SATURDAY 14th OCTOBER 1961

In the programme – priced sixpence – versus Luton Town, News of the World's Harry Ditton wrote about the new European Cup competition: 'Many of these Continentals carry gamesmanship to the point of downright cheating – time-wasting, shirt pulling and obstruction tactics – and matters are not helped by the importation of foreign referees who, by our own standards, are often incompetent'.

WEDNESDAY 14th OCTOBER 1998

Albion fanzine Scars and Stripes hosted 'Fans and Bands United' at the Paradox, West Street, Brighton. The Levellers, Buster Bloodvessel and the Fish Brothers performed to over 1,000 Albion fans. The event raised over £4,000 for the club.

SATURDAY 15th OCTOBER 1932

Albion's unusual FA Cup run continued with a 7-1 home demolition of Worthing in the second qualifying round after the tie was switched from Woodside Road. A crowd of 5,952 watched as George Ansell, Bobby Farrell, Tug Wilson, Arthur Attwood (2) and Potter Smith (2) registered for the Albion.

SATURDAY 15th OCTOBER 1955

Striker Peter Harburn started his amazing goalscoring run – 12 goals in 8 games – in the 3-0 third division (south) victory at Watford. By a quirk of fixture-list fate, it was the second of three games between the clubs on this date. The first, in 1921, finished 1-1 at the Goldstone and the third, in Hertfordshire, ended with the same scoreline in 1988.

TUESDAY 15th OCTOBER 1996

A 1-0 defeat to Hereford United was memorable for the mass walk-out with 15 minutes of the game remaining by fans disillusioned with the board. Most of the 3,444 spectators left when a rocket was set off from behind the East Terrace. The result on the pitch kept Albion four points adrift at the bottom of the basement division.

Friday 16th October 1970

Peter O'Sullivan started the first of 194 consecutive Albion appearances in the 1-0 Division Three defeat at Torquay United.

Saturday 16th October 1984

Winger Steve Penney made his Northern Ireland debut in the 3-0 victory over Israel in Belfast.

Saturday 16th October 1985

Sean Edwards enjoyed the shortest of Albion careers. For his one and only appearance, the Hastings-born full-back replaced the injured Chris Hutchings with just eight minutes remaining of the Full Members Cup group match versus Crystal Palace at Selhurst Park. The 3-1 triumph was secured through strikes from Kieran O'Regan, Danny Wilson and on-loan Martin Keown in front of a paltry 2,207 spectators.

Saturday 16th October 1998

Ecovert South, the managers of Withdean, said the Albion's return to Brighton is unlikely before March 1999.

Saturday 17th October 1981

Albion drew 3-3 with Liverpool at the Goldstone. Ray Kennedy, Kenny Dalglish and Terry McDermott were on target for the Reds. Steve Foster, Jimmy Case and Andy Ritchie replied for the Seagulls.

Friday 17th October 1997

An Albion delegation descended on Woking Football Club to investigate the possibility of a ground-share arrangement with the Conference side.

Wednesday 17th October 2001

The second Peter Taylor to manage Albion took control at the club, replacing Micky Adams.

Tuesday 17th October 2006

An amazing eight of the starting 11 against Boston United, in the Johnstone's Paint Trophy, had come through the Albion's Centres of Excellence.

SATURDAY 18th OCTOBER 1902

Albion enjoyed the biggest away win in the club's history. Shoreham FC are humbled 12-0 in a FA Cup second qualifying round fixture at Oxen Field. The dozen goals come from Ben Garfield, Barney Lee (2), Sid Thair (3), Frank Scott (4), an own-goal and Alf Harland.

FRIDAY 18th OCTOBER 1996

Portsmouth FC confirmed they would not allow Albion to share Fratton Park from 1997 onwards. Albion chief executive David Bellotti responded by announcing that negotiations are proceeding with Gillingham and two unnamed London clubs.

WEDNESDAY 18th OCTOBER 2000

Albion's record run of league games without conceding a goal came to an end against Hartlepool United at Withdean – Michel Kuipers carried the ball over the line just before half-time from a high cross! It didn't matter; Gary Hart, Bobby Zamora (2) and Richard Carpenter netted for a 4-2 win to send the Seagulls up to second in Division Three.

TUESDAY 18th OCTOBER 2005

On-loan Manchester United defender Paul McShane scored the only goal of the game, with 12 minutes remaining, to give the Seagulls their first win over Crystal Palace at Selhurst Park since 1983. The 3,500-plus visiting supporters were on tenterhooks as Clinton Morrison stabbed a loose ball home in the final seconds only for the referee to rule the effort out for off-side.

WEDNESDAY 19th OCTOBER 1983

Jimmy Melia resigned as manager of Brighton & Hove Albion. The Scouser had led his team out at Wembley just five months earlier. His 39-game record reads: 9 wins, 13 draws and 17 losses.

MONDAY 19th OCTOBER 1998

Ian Culverhouse was signed by Albion manager Brian Horton...five days after being released! A change in tactics brought on the turnaround – the experienced defender was to be used as a sweeper.

SATURDAY 20th OCTOBER 1923

Five years after the end of World War I, a memorial to those who died was unveiled in the Goldstone boardroom. It commemorated nine former players and the groundsman Fred Bates.

FRIDAY 20th OCTOBER 1967

Due to a railway guards' dispute, a convoy of four cars ferries Albion players to a Nottingham hotel in readiness for the following day's fixture with Mansfield Town.

SATURDAY 20th OCTOBER 1973

Dave Busby – who went to school with Frank Bruno in Heathfield – made his debut in the 2-0 home win over Shrewsbury Town. The striker was the first black player to feature in Albion's first team.

SATURDAY 20th OCTOBER 1984

The day many Albion fans had been waiting for – the new roof on the North Stand! The crowd of just 10,000 didn't exactly 'raise' the new £200,000 structure during a turgid 0-0 stalemate with Barnsley. The first thousand entrants to the stand were given a free foam hand, leftovers from the FA Cup Final appearance 18 months earlier. Gary Howlett, provider of the first goal on that memorable day, made his last appearance for the club. The game was so poor that manager Chris Cattlin fined himself a week's wages!

SATURDAY 21st OCTOBER 1922

Ernest 'Tug' Wilson made his Albion debut during the 2-1 home win over Brentford. Rejected four years earlier by Sheffield Wednesday for being too small, the little Yorkshireman dominated the left flank for 14 years. Notching up 71 goals in an incredible 566 appearances – a record unlikely ever to be beaten – Tug was much loved by the Goldstone faithful and missed just 29 games in 12 seasons. He set up a bookmakers, with former team-mate Frank Brett, on his retirement.

WEDNESDAY 21st OCTOBER 1998

A Football League Appeals Tribunal awarded Albion more than £1 million compensation from Aston Villa for 17-year-old Gareth Barry. The schoolboy from Hastings attended the club's Centre of Excellence.

SUNDAY 22nd OCTOBER 1879

Harry Kent was born in Warwickshire. The half-back scored 16 times in 151 Albion starts before joining Middlesbrough in 1908.

SATURDAY 22nd OCTOBER 1910

Millwall opened their new ground, The Den, with a 1-0 defeat to Albion. The match – which was watched by 25,000, the biggest crowd to see Brighton until 1937 – was the club's eighth straight victory.

SATURDAY 22nd OCTOBER 1977

An all-ticket Goldstone crowd of 28,208 witnessed a thrilling 1-1 draw with Crystal Palace. Ian 'Spider' Mellor put Albion ahead (40) only for Paul Hinshelwood – brother of Martin and father of Paul – to equalise with eight minutes remaining.

SATURDAY 22nd OCTOBER 1983

It was Chris Cattlin's first game in charge. The former left-back, who made 114 appearances (scoring twice) in four years at the Goldstone, took over from Jimmy Melia. In the following campaign, his shrewd dealings resulted in Albion finishing just a game away from a return to the top flight in 1985. Only the club's second FA Cup sixth round appearance the next season wasn't enough, and the Rock Shop owner was shown the door – much to the disgust of many fans – for the return of former manager Alan Mullery...

SATURDAY 23rd OCTOBER 1920

Jack Doran – who scored 55 goals in just 85 Albion starts – made his international debut for Ireland against England at Roker Park. The Belfast-born hitman failed to find the target in the 2-0 Home Championship defeat.

SATURDAY 23rd OCTOBER 1982

A hero returned to the club. Goldstone darling Peter Ward, who had moved to Nottingham Forest two years earlier, for a fee of £450,000, was brought back on loan for four months and played his first game in the 3-1 first division victory over West Ham United. The nimble striker's appearance attracted a gate of 20,490 – an increase of over eight thousand on the previous home gate.

SATURDAY 24th OCTOBER 1925

Paul Mooney made his debut in the 2-1 third division (south) win over QPR. The dependable stopper, who represented the Albion 315 times, scoring on 11 occasions, was great in the air and once scored a header from the half-way line at Walsall! 'Cast Iron Head' joined County League Vernon Athletic in 1936.

SATURDAY 24th OCTOBER 1987

Ever-present so far that season, popular goalkeeper John Keeley revealed a couple of his personal favourites in a question-and-answer session printed in the club programme for the match versus Brentford. Drink: lager; TV show: *Only Fools & Horses*.

SATURDAY 24th OCTOBER 1998

Nigerian Emeka Ifejiagwa scored in the first of two loan appearances from Charlton Athletic – on this day it was the game's only goal at Barnet's Underhill.

SATURDAY 25th OCTOBER 1930

Just 1,621 spectators watched the short-lived Thames FC play out a 0-0 draw with Albion, at the huge greyhound stadium in West Ham.

SATURDAY 25th OCTOBER 1952

Dennis Foreman scored in his first Albion appearance: the 4-2 home win over Aldershot. The South African-born left-sided attacker managed 69 strikes in 219 games before a bad injury in 1958 slowed down his career for his last years at the Goldstone. He also represented Sussex at cricket from 1952 to 1967. The game is also notable for the debut of Maurice McLafferty. The Scot joined Sheffield United from St. Mirren in 1951 and arrived in Hove for a £1,000 fee a year later. The defender had the unenviable task of competing with Jimmy Langley from 1954 and moved into Sussex County League football.

WEDNESDAY 25th OCTOBER 1978

Winger Peter O'Sullivan came off the bench to score in the last of three appearances for Wales as an Albion player – in the 7-0 thrashing of Malta at Wrexham.

SATURDAY 26th OCTOBER 1996

Over 1,000 Albion fans marched from Brighton Station – via Western Road and Church Road – to the Goldstone Ground in a peaceful demonstration against Bill Archer, Greg Stanley and David Bellotti. The latter was forced from his seat after a firework was thrown during the 0-0 draw with Fulham.

SATURDAY 26th OCTOBER 2002

Albion lost 5-0 at Crystal Palace – with nearly 5,000 away fans present – in the first league meeting between the sides in 13 years.

SATURDAY 27th OCTOBER 1979

The first-team squad attended a Leo Sayer concert at the Brighton Centre after meeting the pint-sized pop star on a pre-season tour of the US.

SATURDAY 27th OCTOBER 1990

Brian McKenna, an 18-year-old Irishman, let in four goals during his one and only Albion appearance: a 4-2 home defeat to Middlesbrough. Dean Wilkins and Mike Small scored Brighton's goals.

SATURDAY 28th OCTOBER 1995

George Parris scored a cheeky goal against Bristol Rovers. As the opposition keeper gathered the ball after an Albion attack ended, the former West Ham man's momentum kept him going off the pitch, so he waited, with his hand on the post, until unsuspecting Pirates' stopper Andy Collett rolled the ball out. He then robbed the ball from the custodian and slotted it into an empty net!

SATURDAY 28th OCTOBER 2000

Lee Steele scored his first goal for Albion after a summer move from Shrewsbury Town. It was the winning goal in a 2-1 victory at Darlington. Nathan Jones opened the scoring for Albion after four minutes, the home side hit back, before Steele struck the winner.

FRIDAY 28th OCTOBER 2005

Deputy Prime Minister John Prescott's letter arrived at Albion HQ regarding the Falmer decision and it's a yes – however, Albion later learn the decision is revoked due to a technical error in the letter's wording.

SATURDAY 29th OCTOBER 1910

'Pom Pom' Bob Whiting ended his record of five straight clean sheets in the 2-1 Goldstone victory over Queens Park Rangers. This was the last match in a fine run of nine consecutive wins, during which only three goals were conceded and eighteen scored.

SATURDAY 29th OCTOBER 1932

The majority of the healthy crowd of 7,723 at Hastings & St. Leonards go home unhappy as Albion ran riot in a 9-0 FA Cup third qualifying round thrashing.

MONDAY 29th OCTOBER 1990

Following a successful tour of the Soviet Union at the end of the previous season, a party of 30 players and officials arrived at the Goldstone Ground from Dinamo Minsk. Mike Small netted for the Albion but goals from Sokol and Kashentseu handed a 2-1 to the Belarussians in front of 1,063 fans. Minsk's striker Igor Gurinovich moved to Hove and scored twice in six appearances.

SATURDAY 30th OCTOBER 1926

Jack Jenkins played his eighth and final game for Wales against Scotland in Glasgow. The full-back held the record for international appearances while an Albion player, until Mark Lawrenson surpassed his tally in April 1980.

SATURDAY 31st OCTOBER 1903

Distinguised soldier Alan Haig-Brown made the first of his three Albion appearances in the 4-0 defeat at West Ham United. The outside-right was also an accomplished writer, penning articles for *The Times* and other newspapers; plus more than a thousand poems and three books; *Sporting Sonnets*, *My Game Book* and *The OTC in the Great War*.

WEDNESDAY 31st OCTOBER 1973

It was not announced officially until the following day, but Brian Clough and Peter Taylor signed a five-year contract with Albion to take control of the team. The pair had just left Derby County – where they led the Rams to the Football League Championship – in a move that shocked the football world.

Brighton & Hove Albion
ON THIS DAY

November

SATURDAY 1st NOVEMBER 1902

Grays United visited the Goldstone for a FA Cup third qualifying round tie. The Essex side stormed into a 4-1 half-time lead but Albion fought back with goals from Ben Garfield, Barney Lee (2), Frank Scott and Jock Caldwell to give an eventual final scoreline of 5-5 – still the highest-scoring draw in the club's history!

SATURDAY 1st NOVEMBER 1924

Watford were the Goldstone visitors as Reg Wilkinson made his Albion debut. The Norwich-born right-half played in his hometown club's first-ever league fixture in 1920 and went on to play over 100 games for the Canaries before being sold to Sunderland for £250 in 1923. For 10 seasons from 1924, Reg was first choice in Charlie Webb's line-up and went on to score 16 goals in 396 Albion games.

FRIDAY 1st NOVEMBER 1968

Following Archie Macaulay's resignation, the board appointed a 'selection committee', including the skipper Nobby Lawton, to pick the side. The process was used for two games, both of which ended in defeat.

SATURDAY 1st NOVEMBER 2003

New manager Mark McGhee took charge of his first game, the 2-2 Division Two draw at Peterborough United.

SATURDAY 2nd NOVEMBER 1929

Walsall-born Dave Walker made his first Albion appearance at Northampton Town's County Ground. The former railway worker took three seasons before finding his ideal position – wing-half – and went on to feature 349 times, scoring 30 goals.

TUESDAY 2nd NOVEMBER 1993

'Gulls Eye' appealed for fans to attend what might be the club's last-ever game, against Wrexham in the second division. Just 5,530 turn up.

SATURDAY 2nd NOVEMBER 1996

Denny Mundee (pen), Jeff Minton and captain Mark Morris scored the goals in Albion's 3-2 win at Hartlepool. It would be the only away victory of the season!

SATURDAY 3rd NOVEMBER 1973

New manager Brian Clough and his assistant Peter Taylor were applauded as they took their seats in the directors' box. The crowd of 16,017 for the third division visit of York City is nearly 10,000 up on the previous attendance.

TUESDAY 3rd NOVEMBER 1993

Albion were in the High Court to fight off a winding-up petition from the Inland Revenue and Customs & Excise.

FRIDAY 4th NOVEMBER 1960

Albion splashed out a record £15,000 for 22-year-old Tony Nicholas from Chelsea. The forward topped the scoring charts at the end of his first season – 13 in 27 starts – but was part of George Curtis's cull in 1962 after relegation to the third division.

SATURDAY 4th NOVEMBER 1978

Peter Ward was dropped for the second division encounter at Sheffield United. His deputy, Malcolm Poskett, scored the only goal of the game to move Alan Mullery's men up to eighth.

SATURDAY 4th NOVEMBER 2000

A Withdean then-record crowd of 6,746 was in attendance for the 4-1 third division victory over Carlisle United.

SATURDAY 5th NOVEMBER 1921

Jack Doran smashed five past a hapless Northampton Town in a 7-0 Goldstone win. Bill McAllister also grabbed two in the victory.

WEDNESDAY 5th NOVEMBER 1997

Just 1,025, the lowest ever gate for an Albion 'home' fixture in the Football League, are at Priestfield for the visit of Barnet, who record an easy 3-0 win to leave Steve Gritt's men in 23rd spot in the bottom division, six points above Doncaster Rovers.

SATURDAY 5th NOVEMBER 2005

Albion went down 3-0 in a Championship contest at Stoke City's Britannia Stadium.

SATURDAY 6th NOVEMBER 1976

A third successive victory was achieved with a 4-0 home win over Swindon Town. Andy Rollings, Ian Mellor (2) and Peter Ward are on target to keep Albion at the top of the third division.

SATURDAY 6th NOVEMBER 1982

Albion – unbeaten in their first six home Division One fixtures of the season – hosted Manchester United. The record continued as Peter Ward grabbed the only goal of the contest.

SATURDAY 6th NOVEMBER 1993

Kurt Nogan scored his 10th goal of the season in the 1-0 win at Craven Cottage.

SATURDAY 7th NOVEMBER 1931

Late-starter Arthur Attwood pulled on an Albion shirt for the first time in the 3-2 home defeat by Fulham. The centre-forward was 26 when he made his Football League debut for Walsall. He headed south-east from Bristol Rovers aged 29, and an impressive 75 goals in 104 starts is still the best goals-to-games ratio in the history of the club.

TUESDAY 7th NOVEMBER 1978

Albion earned an away tie with champions Nottingham Forest in the League Cup quarter-final after beating Peterborough United, thanks to a Mark Lawrenson goal, in front of 21,421 at the Goldstone.

SATURDAY 7th NOVEMBER 1981

The programme for the Birmingham City match explained that a fox had been digging up the pitch and eating goal nets. A marksman from a local pest control firm took out the offending animal with one shot.

SATURDAY 7th NOVEMBER 1998

Gary Hart and Jeff Minton were both on the scoresheet as Albion produced a brilliant second-half performance to turn a 1-0 deficit into a 2-1 win. Albion's travelling fans had to wait until the 70th minute for Hart to cancel out Glen Naylor's 17th-minute opening goal. Then two minutes later Albion were awarded a penalty, which was converted from the spot by Minton.

FRIDAY 8th NOVEMBER 1957

Alan Curbishley – real name Llewellyn – was born in East Ham, London. After spells at Birmingham City, Aston Villa and Charlton Athletic, the midfielder moved to Brighton in 1987. Curbs netted on 15 occasions in 132 Albion appearances before a move back to Charlton in 1990.

SATURDAY 8th NOVEMBER 1975

Albion's 2-0 third division Goldstone victory over Southend United is the club's only win – in 13 attempts – on this date.

TUESDAY 8th NOVEMBER 1983

Just over a week after thrashing Bury 10-0 in the Milk Cup, West Ham United hosted the Albion at Upton Park in the third round of the competition. The Hammers ran out 1-0 winners.

SATURDAY 9th NOVEMBER 1962

Terry Connor was born in Leeds. In 1983 the striker joined Albion in a direct exchange that took Andy Ritchie to Leeds United in a deal worth £500,000 – a club record fee paid. The 20-year-old was cup-tied for the big day but made his mark the following season back in Division Two, scoring 17 times. Terry hit 59 goals in 174 games before being sold to Portsmouth for £200,000 in 1987.

SATURDAY 9th NOVEMBER 1968

Freddie Goodwin took charge of his first Albion game, a 3-1 win over Bristol Rovers, the club's first win for six games. Kit Napier's hat-trick moved the team up two places to 21st in the third division.

SATURDAY 9th NOVEMBER 1996

Albion fans made the ultimate sacrifice, boycotting their team's home game against Mansfield Town in an effort to bring down the hated regime of Bill Archer, Greg Stanley and David Bellotti. The official attendance was just 1,933, the lowest home gate ever recorded by Albion in the Football League at the time. A gate mysteriously opened on the East Terrace just before half time and hundreds flooded into the ground and took over the directors' box during the interval. The game ended in a 1-1 draw.

MONDAY 10th NOVEMBER 1947

It's a sad day at the Goldstone as two club legends departed. Team manager Tommy Cook left after seven months as boss while Charlie Webb ends his 38-year involvement by quitting as general manager.

SATURDAY 10th NOVEMBER 1979

Ray Kennedy, Kenny Dalglish (2) and David Johnson netted for champions Liverpool during their 4-1 victory in front of 29,682 Goldstone fans.

SATURDAY 10th NOVEMBER 1990

The programme included a centre-page spread of the proposed new stadium. The 25,000 all-seater has space for 5,000 cars with an adjacent full-size astroturf pitch. A site had yet to be found. Commercial director Ray Bloom said: 'We are currently losing £1,000 a day and are very nearly £3m in debt. It's not feasible to convert the Goldstone Ground'.

MONDAY 11th NOVEMBER 1907

Albion played Queens Park Rangers at Park Royal, Middlesex, in a Western (Midweek) League fixture. Played in dense fog, the wingers were only just discernible from behind the spectator ropes. Arthur Hulme scored a penalty for the Albion, allegedly, but five minutes later the game was finally abandoned.

MONDAY 11th NOVEMBER 2002

Steve Sidwell made his Albion debut on loan from Arsenal, as a 19-year-old, in the 1-1 televised first division draw at Wolverhampton Wanderers.

SATURDAY 11th NOVEMBER 2006

Northwich Victoria visited Withdean for this FA Cup first round tie. The Conference side didn't stand a chance as Albion turned on the style and rattled in eight goals without reply. Jake Robinson grabbed his second hat-trick in a fortnight; Alex Revell and Dean Cox both registered a brace while Joe Gatting scored his first Albion goal, as did left-back Sam Rents. The victory sent Albion through to a second-round tie with Stafford Rangers.

SATURDAY 12th NOVEMBER 1994

In front of 3,815 fans, Albion were humiliated by Diadora Isthmian League side Kingstonian in south London – the home side won 2-1.

SATURDAY 12th NOVEMBER 1995

Junior McDougald scored both the goals during Albion's 2-2 FA Cup first round draw at Essex non-leaguers Canvey Island.

SATURDAY 13th NOVEMBER 1965

Albion romped to their finest cup (proper) victory. Southern Division One outfit Wisbech Town were the Goldstone Ground visitors for this FA Cup first round tie. Albion were three up at the interval with strikes from Charlie Livesey, Jack Smith and an own-goal. Then the floodgates opened: Goodchild, Collins, Cassidy (2), Smith again, Gould and Livesey again made it 10-1 to the Albion!

SATURDAY 13th NOVEMBER 1976

Albion legend Steve Foster scored his first 'goal' in professional football for Portsmouth; a 20-yard header against Bury… into his own net.

SATURDAY 13th NOVEMBER 2004

It's reunion time with Bobby Zamora as Albion visit Upton Park for a Championship clash. Steve Claridge – at 38 – makes his Albion debut. Guy Butters heads the winner with 20 minutes remaining.

SATURDAY 14th NOVEMBER 1931

Arthur Attwood began an amazing scoring sequence – 14 goals in eight games – by netting in an 2-1 win at Thames.

SATURDAY 14th NOVEMBER 1992

Hayes were swept aside 2-0 in this FA Cup first round victory. Andy Kennedy and Robert Codner got the goals.

SATURDAY 14th NOVEMBER 1998

Over 4,000 Albion fans were present in the 7,406 crowd at Leyton Orient's Brisbane Road for this FA Cup first round tie. Richie Barker opened the scoring but the Londoners responded by netting four before Kerry Mayo notched a consolation to make it 4-2.

SATURDAY 15th NOVEMBER 1997

Revenge was on the cards after Albion relegated Hereford United back in May. The FA Cup first round tie at Edgar Street was the main game on *Match of the Day*. Stuart Storer fired the away side into the lead. It didn't last – a Neil Grayson double sent the Bulls through.

SATURDAY 15th NOVEMBER 2003

It was Mark McGhee's first home game in charge, against Bristol City. Not a good start; the Robins won 4-1.

MONDAY 16th NOVEMBER 1953

Graham Moseley was born in Lancashire. The keeper featured just 44 times for Derby County in six years and was signed by Alan Mullery for £20,000 in November 1977 to compete with Eric Steele. In a topsy-turvy Albion career, Graham was in and out of the side and was considered a bit clumsy – after incidents with a hedge-trimmer and a glass window. Despite this, the stopper was immensely popular at the Goldstone and was between the sticks for both Cup Final appearances. A thoroughly deserved 'Player of the Season' accolade came his way after Albion came close to regaining their first division status in 1984/85. It was followed by a campaign of sharing duties with Perry Digweed. A free transfer to Cardiff City beckoned before a car crash ended his career in 1988.

WEDNESDAY 16th NOVEMBER 1983

Albion defender Kieran O'Regan played for the Republic of Ireland in their 8-0 thrashing of Malta, a Euro qualifier in Dublin.

SATURDAY 17th NOVEMBER 1945

After six seasons, the FA Cup returned to the football season… in a unique, two-legged format. Albion won the first leg – at home against Romford – 3-1 at the Goldstone Ground with goals from Jock Davie (2) and Frank Hindley.

SATURDAY 17th NOVEMBER 1979

European champions Nottingham Forest hosted the Albion at the City Ground. Forest hadn't lost at home in the league for over two seasons. Brighton had never won an away fixture in the first division… Gerry Ryan's goal earned two points to lift Albion off the bottom.

SATURDAY 17th NOVEMBER 2001

Shrewsbury Town were the Withdean visitors for this FA Cup first round tie. The third successive victory by the same scoreline, and goalscorer, is achieved courtesy of a solitary strike by Bobby Zamora after 31 minutes in front of 5,450 spectators.

SATURDAY 18th NOVEMBER 1972

Local boy Steve Piper donned the stripes for the first time. The 1-0 home defeat to Burnley – the start of a 13-match losing streak – wasn't an ideal start for Brighton-born Piper. But steady performances endeared him to the fans and he was ever-present during the promotion campaign of 1976/77. After nine strikes in 190 games, Steve moved to Portsmouth for £20,000 in February 1978 after losing his place to Paul Clark.

SATURDAY 18th NOVEMBER 2000

Micky Adams's men smashed six past Aldershot Town in the FA Cup first round with strikes from Richard Carpenter, Charlie Oatway, Bobby Zamora and Matthew Wicks – plus two penalties from Paul Watson – to give them a 6-2 victory at the Recreation Ground.

SATURDAY 18th NOVEMBER 2006

The programme reports on a visit of Albion's community scheme staff to Tanzania for the 'Coaching For Hope' conference. The project uses football to educate on the dangers of HIV and AIDS across Africa.

SATURDAY 19th NOVEMBER 1955

Newport County were on the receiving end of a FA Cup first round beating at the Goldstone Ground. Four strikes from Peter Harburn, a hat-trick from Denis Foreman and a goal from Frankie Howard added up to an 8-1 reverse for the Welshmen.

WEDNESDAY 19th NOVEMBER 1980

Michael Robinson scored on his second appearance for the Republic of Ireland in a 6-0 thumping of Cyprus in a World Cup qualifier.

TUESDAY 19th NOVEMBER 1996

Just 58 Albion fans headed west to Swansea. The third division fixture ended in defeat for Jimmy Case's men.

SATURDAY 20th NOVEMBER 1971

It was FA Cup first round day at the Goldstone Ground. Southern League Premier Division Hillingdon Borough lost 7-1.

SATURDAY 20th NOVEMBER 1976

Just under 30,000 fans crammed into the Goldstone to see Peter Ward and Ian Mellor score in Albion's 2-2 draw FA Cup first round draw with Crystal Palace.

SATURDAY 21st NOVEMBER 1981

Michael Robinson is felled by a metal object thrown from the North Stand at the Goldstone Ground. Albion come back from 2-0 down against Notts County – with goals from Jimmy Case and Steve Gatting – to draw 2-2 in front of 13,854 supporters. Mickey Thomas made his first full appearance for the club.

TUESDAY 21st NOVEMBER 1995

Jimmy Case's Albion managerial career peaks… in his first game in charge! Canvey Island were brushed aside 4-1 in a FA Cup replay but the team eventually succumbed to relegation to the basement division as off the pitch goings-on went from bad to terrible. The former player was sacked in December 1996 after 32 defeats in 57 games.

SATURDAY 22nd NOVEMBER 1975

The dawn of a new era; a specially-chartered train took 584 Albion fans to Watford for a first round FA Cup tie. It was the first of the 'Seagull Specials' that would transport supporters across the country. Neil Martin and Fred Binney (2) were on target in the 3-0 victory.

SATURDAY 22nd NOVEMBER 1980

Alan Mullery's Albion side were beaten 4-1 by Manchester United in front of 23,277 spectators at the Goldstone. Andy Ritchie scored his first goal for the Seagulls against his former club.

SATURDAY 22nd NOVEMBER 1952

FA Cup giant-killing specialists Yeovil Town host Albion on their sloping pitch at The Huish. Frankie Howard, Les Owens (2) and a Des Tennant penalty earns a 4-1 win and second round tie with Norwich City.

SATURDAY 23rd NOVEMBER 1957

Dave Sexton notched a hat-trick as Albion disposed of Crystal Palace 4-2 in front of 15,757 fans at Selhurst Park.

SATURDAY 23rd NOVEMBER 1996

Carlisle United beat Albion 3-1 at the Goldstone in front of a pitiful crowd of just 4,155. The game marked the first appearance of Kerry Mayo. The local lad came up through the ranks and began his career during the club's lowest ebb. He celebrated his testimonial season in 2006/07.

SATURDAY 24th NOVEMBER 1973

A full house of 6,500 were present at Walton & Hersham's Stompond Lane for Albion's FA Cup first round visit. Brian Clough's professionals could not overcome the amateurs. The 0-0 draw meant a replay.

THURSDAY 24th NOVEMBER 1977

Alan Mullery paid Fulham £238,000 for the services of striker Teddy Maybank, a club record.

SATURDAY 24th NOVEMBER 1990

The programme versus Millwall (0-0 draw) reflected on Albion's record-breaking goalscoring season of 1955/56; 121 goals in all competitions included wins by four or more goals on an amazing 12 occasions, and victories of 6-0 over Norwich City and 8-1 over Newport County.

SATURDAY 25th NOVEMBER 1950

Don Welsh's Albion side – having conceded 13 goals in their previous two league games – faced a potential FA Cup first round banana skin at Tooting & Mitcham United. Thankfully, the majority of the 10,000 crowd went home disappointed as Albion won 3-2.

SATURDAY 25th NOVEMBER 1961

Bobby Baxter made his first Albion appearance during the 0-0 home draw with Preston North End. The left-back was a consistent fixture in the side for six seasons after scoring 30 times in 67 run-outs as a striker for Darlington. Bobby arrived in a swap deal for Dennis Windross in August 1961 and performed admirably 220 times for Albion, netting on seven occasions, before heading west to Torquay United in 1967.

SATURDAY 26th NOVEMBER 1955

Albion take a break from their goalscoring exploits; well, off the peddle a little! In the previous three games they have notched 4-0, 5-0 and 8-1 victories. On this occasion, the opposition get in on the act as Colchester United manage three in a six-goal thriller at Layer Road.

SATURDAY 26th NOVEMBER 1994

Ade Akinbiyi made his first appearance for Albion in the 2-1 defeat at Brentford. The 20-year-old striker netted four times in seven starts and went on to be involved in transfers with fees totalling nearly £16m.

TUESDAY 26th NOVEMBER 1996

An awful night for the Albion. The club's last ever FA Cup tie at the Goldstone – a home replay to Sudbury Town – was lost 4-3 in a penalty shoot-out after a 1-1 scoreline after extra-time.

SATURDAY 27th NOVEMBER 1965

Albion thrashed Southend United 9-1 in a third division clash – just a fortnight after putting one more past Wisbech Town! The goals – in front of 11,124 home fans – came from Jimmy Collins, Johnny Goodchild (2), Wally Gould, Jack Smith (3) and Charlie Livesey (2).

SATURDAY 27th NOVEMBER 1971

Kit Napier scored a cheeky Goldstone goal against Chesterfield. The opposition goalkeeper thought he'd been awarded a free-kick in his area and placed the ball accordingly. As the other players awaited the kick Napier realised the ref had not blown his whistle and promptly scored!

SATURDAY 27th NOVEMBER 1982

Albion lost 2-0 at home to Notts County. The visitors are the only club Brighton have faced in every division they've played in: One, Two, Three, Three (South) and Four.

SATURDAY 27th NOVEMBER 2004

Albion went to Ipswich hoping to end their wretched run of results there. On the five previous encounters on this date, the Seagulls had lost! Unfortunately, the hex continued as Ipswich Town won 1-0 in front of almost 27,000 fans at Portman Road.

SATURDAY 28th NOVEMBER 1931

Folkestone hosted Albion in Kent for this FA Cup first round fixture. The Sussex side came away 5-2 winners.

SATURDAY 28th NOVEMBER 1953

One of Albion's greatest-ever goalscorers, Albert Mundy, found the net on his debut versus Bristol City. Nearly 20,000 fans were inside the Goldstone to see the 2-1 win.

WEDNESDAY 28th NOVEMBER 1973

Named after the whole QPR squad, Anthony Philip David Terry Frank Donald Stanley Gerry Gordon Stephen James Oatway was born in Hammersmith, London. When his aunt was told of the proposed name she proclaimed "he'd look a right Charlie" and the nickname stuck. The tough-tackling midfielder arrived from Brentford for a £10,000 fee in July 1999 and played a huge part in the successive championships of 2000/01 and 2001/02. A broken ankle – ironically at home to QPR on Boxing Day 2005 – eventually ended the popular player's career in August 2007, after nearly two years of trying to battle back to fitness. Charlie featured 224 times for Albion, scoring nine times.

SATURDAY 28th NOVEMBER 1981

The 2-0 defeat at Manchester United was the Albion's 100th game in the top flight.

SATURDAY 29th NOVEMBER 1969

News that Albion's home game with Torquay United had been postponed because of the blizzard reaches British Rail and notices were posted at Brighton and Hove Stations. They were wrong! The 5,640 fans who made it to the Goldstone – nearly 6,000 down on the average – saw the teams fight out a 2-2 draw in the snow.

FRIDAY 29th NOVEMBER 1996

Bill Archer announced his agreement to the Football Association's suggestion of arbitration in an attempt to reach a deal with Dick Knight's consortium. It was also disclosed that the club had signed a two-year deal to share Gillingham's Priestfield Stadium from 1997, with an option for a third season.

SATURDAY 30th NOVEMBER 1901

Albion enjoyed their first meeting with a team destined to become a fellow Football League side. Fulham were the visitors to the County Ground and Clem Barker and Frank McAvoy scored the goals to take the Southern League points in front of 1,900 Hove fans.

SATURDAY 30th NOVEMBER 1946

Norwich City walloped the Albion 7-2 at Carrow Road in the FA Cup first round to avenge their 4-1 Goldstone defeat at the third round stage the previous season.

SATURDAY 30th NOVEMBER 1996

Another day, another protest. This time London was the location as around 800 Albion fans marched from Victoria Station to Marble Arch to deliver a 5,726-name petition to the FA calling for chairman Bill Archer and chief executive David Bellotti to be charged with misconduct likely to bring the game into disrepute. A few hours later, Albion lost 2-0 at Fulham's Craven Cottage.

Brighton & Hove Albion
ON THIS DAY

DECEMBER

WEDNESDAY 1st DECEMBER 1909

It was a rough-and-tumble contest at the Goldstone Ground. Bullet Jones was sent off (very rare in those days) after both of Norwich's goalkeepers had left the pitch as a result of collisions with the powerful forward. George Featherstone (2), Bert Longstaff (2) and Bill Hastings were on target in the 5-0 drubbing in front of just 2,000 fans in Hove.

SATURDAY 1st DECEMBER 1973

Albion were the first team to put two past Bristol Rovers this season in the third division fixture at the Goldstone Ground – unfortunately the Gas got eight! The Pirates were flying in the league and were coming to the end of a 22-match unbeaten run. It was Brian Powney's last time between the sticks and the ITV *Big Match* cameras were on hand to record the humiliation for posterity.

SATURDAY 1st DECEMBER 2001

Bobby Zamora sealed the points in a 2-0 win at Bury with a wonderful strike. The striker picked up the ball on the half-way line and laid it off to Paul Brooker. The pass back was timed to perfection and as Shakers' defender Michael Nelson closed in, Bobby chipped the ball over the advancing goalkeeper from well outside the area.

SATURDAY 2nd DECEMBER 2000

Another wonder strike from Bobby Zamora – this time at Withdean. The ball was sliced high into the air in Halifax Town's box. The prolific forward anticipated, kept his eye on the ball and smashed in an unstoppable volley a foot off the ground across the goalkeeper and in at the far post – a quite stunning strike. The game finished 2-0.

SATURDAY 3rd DECEMBER 1983

Danny Wilson endeared himself to Albion fans by scoring twice on his debut; the 3-1 second division Goldstone win over Cardiff City.

TUESDAY 3rd DECEMBER 1996

Hated chief executive David Bellotti was driven from the West Stand directors' box for the last time as fans surged across the pitch from the North Stand. It made no difference as Albion lost 3-2 at home to Darlington to fall nine points adrift at the foot of the bottom division.

WEDNESDAY 4th DECEMBER 1935

Four days earlier, Cheltenham Town – in their first Southern League season – did well to hold third division (south) Albion to a goalless Goldstone draw in the FA Cup first round. The replay doesn't go quite as well for the Gloucestershire outfit as their guests netted six times – Alec Law (3), Bert Stephens (2) and Bobby Farrell – without reply.

SATURDAY 4th DECEMBER 1948

The Goldstone gate of 22,994 was the highest ever for a home league encounter at the time. Albion overcame Notts County to win 3-2.

WEDNESDAY 4th DECEMBER 1996

Playing legend Jimmy Case was sacked as manager following the disastrous Goldstone defeat at home to Darlington the previous night.

SATURDAY 5th DECEMBER 1981

Despite being unbeaten at home in the league since the first game of the season – a run of eight games – only 14,251 fans were at the Goldstone for the 2-1 victory over Sunderland.

SATURDAY 5th DECEMBER 1987

Kevin Bremner and Garry Nelson scored as Albion went through to Round Three of the FA Cup with a 2-1 win at Northampton Town.

SATURDAY 6th DECEMBER 1919

Zach March bagged a hat-trick in a 3-2 Southern League Goldstone victory. The little Sussex-born winger gained fame shortly before his passing – aged 101 – in 1994, when he was identified as the country's oldest surviving former professional footballer.

MONDAY 6th DECEMBER 1976

At the third time of asking, the first round FA Cup tie between Albion and Palace was resolved at Stamford Bridge. Palace took the lead before referee Ron Challis awarded Albion a penalty. Brian Horton scored, only for Challis to order a retake, which was then saved by Paul Hammond. At the end, Alan Mullery became involved in a heated debate with Challis, made a two-fingered gesture at Palace fans, and flung money in a puddle shouting "You're not worth that, Palace!" He was fined £75.

SATURDAY 7th DECEMBER 1963

Half-back Dave Turner made his Albion debut in the 2-0 Goldstone fourth division victory over Darlington. Wholehearted in the tackle, and popular with both players and supporters, Dave spent a decade from 1980 as chief coach of the Toronto Blizzard in Canada after scoring 34 goals in 338 appearances for the Albion.

SATURDAY 7th DECEMBER 1985

The programme for the Barnsley match congratulated 14-year-old Albion fan Simon Rodger, from Shoreham, on winning a 'Bobby Charlton Soccer Skills' competition. His prize was a trip to show off his skills before Manchester United's Old Trafford contest with Ipswich Town. Almost 17 years later, after playing nearly 300 games for Crystal Palace in 12 years, Simon made his debut for his boyhood heroes – in the 5-0 mauling at Selhurst Park!

SATURDAY 8th DECEMBER 1973

Peter Grummitt donned the Albion goalkeeper's jersey for the first time at Prenton Park. Brian Clough took drastic measures after his side had shipped 12 goals in just two matches! Peter arrived after a decade with Nottingham Forest, and he helped Albion to promotion to Division Two in 1977. Sadly, a knee injury ended his career in Hove after 158 starts.

TUESDAY 8th DECEMBER 1981

A first victory in Southampton for 25 years was reward for strikes from Andy Ritchie and Steve Gatting. The 2-0 win moved Mike Bailey's side into sixth place in the first division, a UEFA Cup spot and the club's highest ever league position.

MONDAY 9th DECEMBER 1996

The FA deduct two points from managerless Albion's meagre total as a result of the pitch invasion at the home match with Lincoln City. The club are 11 points adrift at the foot of Division Three.

TUESDAY 9th DECEMBER 1997

Five senior professionals – Craig Maskell, Paul McDonald, Mark Morris, Denny Mundee and John Humphrey – are paid off as Dick Knight struggled to keep the club afloat with low attendances at Gillingham.

SATURDAY 10th DECEMBER 1994

Robert Codner (including a stunning 40-yarder) with two – in his last game for the club – and one from on-loan Ade Akinbiyi sealed a 3-0 win over Plymouth Argyle. It is the club's only ever win on this date.

FRIDAY 10th DECEMBER 1999

The heavens open and soaked-to-the-skin fans – particularly those in Withdean's south stand – witness a 4-3 scoreline. Unfortunately, the result favoured visitors Rochdale. The crowd is a paltry 5,049.

SATURDAY 11th DECEMBER 1982

George Aitken took charge of the first of his 18 games as caretaker boss. The club's only sub-10,000 attendance of the season witnessed a 3-0 win over Norwich City. Later that evening, Irish international Tony Grealish and his wife Pip hosted a party at their Peacehaven home. It was decided that all guests should wear green, otherwise they would be refused entry. Most players wore green pullovers or shirts while Steve Foster wore one green sock. Gerry Ryan's wife Simeon came dressed as a Christmas tree.

SATURDAY 11th DECEMBER 1993

Following the dismissal of Barry Lloyd, Martin Hinshelwood was in control for Albion's 2-2 at Hartlepool United.

WEDNESDAY 11th DECEMBER 1996

Steve Gritt, the then 39-year-old former Charlton Athletic player, was unveiled as new Albion boss.

SATURDAY 12th DECEMBER 1931

Tug Wilson, Arthur Attwood (2, 1 pen), Dan Kirkwood and Bobby Farrell are on target in the 5-0 home win over Doncaster Rovers in the FA Cup second round. Albion have won eight and lost just once on this date, scoring 25 goals and conceding only 10.

SATURDAY 12th DECEMBER 1983

In the programme for the Chester City game, it is announced that: 'Steve and Joy Gatting are celebrating the birth of their first child on November 26. Joe Gatting weighed in at an impressive 7lb 14oz and is set to follow in the footsteps of his footballing dad and cricketing Uncle Mike.'

WEDNESDAY 13th DECEMBER 1978

Two 'Seagull Special' trains broke down en route to Nottingham Forest and missed Albion's first League Cup fifth round appearance. The visitors were not outclassed as the league champions ran out 3-1 winners.

SATURDAY 13th DECEMBER 1980

Goodison Park was the setting for a seven-goal thriller. Peter O'Sullivan, Andy Ritchie and Michael Robinson all scored against Everton but it wasn't enough – Albion lose 4-3.

WEDNESDAY 14th DECEMBER 1932

Manager Charlie Webb described the comeback from 2-0 down to win 3-2 at Wrexham as one of the greatest Albion performances during his 28 years in charge. Bobby Farrell's goal in extra-time secured a home tie against Chelsea in the FA Cup.

MONDAY 14th DECEMBER 1987

Albion midfielder Mike Trusson was beaten by David Gorton during an eye-balling contest at the Junior Seagulls Christmas Party.

SATURDAY 14th DECEMBER 1996

Steve Gritt is welcomed with incorrectly-spelt graffiti at the Goldstone. Only 3,762 fans were present for the 3-0 victory over Hull City. It was the first home win for three months.

WEDNESDAY 15th DECEMBER 1937

Jock Davie scored four as Albion demolished non-league South Liverpool – later Jimmy Case's first club – 6-0 in a FA Cup Goldstone replay. Bert Stephens and Bobby Farrell were also on target.

SATURDAY 15th DECEMBER 1990

WBO middleweight champion Chris Eubank paraded his champion's belt before the Goldstone crowd, prior to the game with Barnsley, to promote his forthcoming fight at the Brighton Centre.

MONDAY 15th DECEMBER 1997

A public meeting at Hove Town Hall formally launched the campaign to secure the use of Withdean as a temporary home for the club.

WEDNESDAY 16th DECEMBER 1914

With the nation at war with Germany, Albion players Archie Needham, Frank Routledge, Frank Spencer and Jack Woodhouse signed up for the 'Footballers' Battalion' of the Middlesex Regiment.

WEDNESDAY 16th DECEMBER 1992

The High Court judge granted the Albion a stay of execution against a winding-up order brought by the Inland Revenue and Customs & Excise. Later that evening, goals from Robert Codner and John Crumplin secured a 2-1 FA Cup replay victory at Woking.

FRIDAY 16th DECEMBER 2005

John Prescott was met with enthusiastic applause from the Withdean faithful after approving the Falmer Stadium decision. Albion beat the Deputy Prime Minister's team, Hull City, 2-1 with goals from Seb Carole and Charlie Oatway. In the programme, fan Gus Nunneley was pictured receiving a signed shirt to commemorate him watching 500 consecutive Albion matches.

WEDNESDAY 17th DECEMBER 1969

Albion finally lost to Walsall in the FA Cup – in a third replay. The Saddlers won 2-1 at Coventry City's Highfield Road.

WEDNESDAY 17th DECEMBER 1980

Despite playing just four minutes for the Albion, Israeli Moshe Gariani represented his country three times while on the south coast – the last of which was a 3-0 defeat to Portugal.

SATURDAY 18th DECEMBER 1982

A stray dog caused havoc on the pitch at Maine Road. The players returned to the dressing-rooms as it took six minutes to catch the animal. On resumption, Andy Ritchie scored in the 1-1 first division draw with Manchester City.

SATURDAY 18th DECEMBER 1993

Liam Brady – PFA Player of the Year in 1979, and winner of two Italian league championships with Juventus – takes charge of his first Albion match, a 1-0 home defeat to Bradford City.

SATURDAY 19th DECEMBER 1981

Match of the Day's 45 staff packed up their equipment and hot-footed it to Stamford Bridge after Albion's home fixture with Leeds United was postponed.

TUESDAY 19th DECEMBER 1984

Manager Chris Cattlin stepped in to help after Hove 13th Scouts lost their kit! The former left-back replaced the old green kit out of his own pocket, with the help of David Rose Sports.

SATURDAY 20th DECEMBER 1958

After a record 9-0 humiliation on their second division debut, Billy Lane's Albion side welcomed Middlesbrough, the victors that day. In a game shown later on BBC TV, Brian Clough, who had scored five at Ayresome Park, grabbed a hat-trick for the visitors while Johnny Shephard netted his second consecutive brace as Brighton went down 6-4. Middlesbrough thus scored 15 goals past Albion that season!

SATURDAY 20th DECEMBER 1980

A first-half strike from Michael Robinson was enough to beat eventual league champions Aston Villa at the Goldstone. The end-of-season table included Ipswich in second; Liverpool fifth; Nottingham Forest seventh; Manchester United eighth; Leeds United ninth; and Chelsea 12th – in Division Two.

SATURDAY 21st DECEMBER 1901

Shoreham-born right-back Ned Collins failed to turn up at Maidenhead for a Southern League second division fixture. Albion played with 10 men yet managed a 3-2 win with goals from Clem Barker and CJ Mendham (2).

SUNDAY 21st DECEMBER 1986

Albion tried to attract a bigger crowd for this Division Two game with Shrewsbury Town. Nearly 1,700 senior citizens and youngsters were admitted free to boost the gate to 8,220 and they were rewarded with a 3-0 win. Barry Lloyd revealed, in the programme, that people say his music taste is boring. His favourites are George Benson and namesake Manilow.

THURSDAY 22nd DECEMBER 1887

Gunner Higham entered the world in Daventry. After initially performing in the reserves, the left-back made his debut in 1908. As a reservist, Gunner was the first Brighton player to be called up on the outbreak of the Great War and subsequently missed the whole of 1914/15. He survived the hostilities and played one more season, 1919/20, before hanging up his boots after one goal in 159 starts.

SATURDAY 22nd DECEMBER 1923

The legendary Tommy Cook swept Bournemouth aside at the Goldstone with four strikes in a 5-0 win. Goalkeeper Billy Hayes started a remarkable run of seven successive clean sheets.

SUNDAY 22nd DECEMBER 1996

Former England goalkeeper Peter Shilton celebrated his 1,000th league appearance against Albion at Leyton Orient. Live on Sky TV, the visitors did their level best to give the veteran as little work to do as possible as the O's ran out 2-0 winners. Hundreds of Seagulls fans protested against the board.

SATURDAY 23rd DECEMBER 1972

Albion lost for the seventh consecutive time. High-flying Queens Park Rangers won 2-1 at the Goldstone to keep Pat Saward's men bottom of the second division. The side lost the next six games too.

MONDAY 24th DECEMBER 1900

Dan Kirkwood was born in Scotland. The striker – signed for £500 from Sheffield Wednesday – formed the most prolific goalscoring partnership in the Albion's history, linking up with Hugh Vallance to score a total of 63 goals in 1929/30. Given a free transfer to Luton Town in 1933, he netted 82 times in just 181 starts.

SATURDAY 24th DECEMBER 1955

The last time Albion played on Christmas Eve is this match in 1955, against Northampton Town at the Goldstone Ground. Dennis Gordon, Albert Mundy, Peter Harburn and Glen Wilson were full of festive cheer, scoring in the 4-0 triumph to give Albion's supporters the perfect early Christmas present.

MONDAY 25th DECEMBER 1922

Albion enjoyed their best win on Christmas Day. Eddie Fuller (2), Abe Jones, Wally Little (pen), Tommy Cook (2) and Andy Neil are on target during a 7-1 trashing of Portsmouth in front of 15,000 spectators at the Goldstone.

WEDNESDAY 25th DECEMBER 1940

With World War II raging, football continued under the auspices of the War South League and the team – all five of them; one senior player, three juniors and (as a guest) Bolton's Jimmy Ithell – travel to Carrow Road. After borrowing some Norwich juniors and servicemen from the crowd, Albion let the Canaries fly to a rather unflattering 18 goals without reply!

THURSDAY 25th DECEMBER 1957

Albion's last ever Christmas Day contest was a 2-2 Goldstone draw with Swindon Town – the third of four games in seven days!

WEDNESDAY 26th DECEMBER 1979

Albion entertained Crystal Palace for the first time in Division One. It's a happy Christmas for the south coast faithful among the 28,358 crowd. A Brian Horton penalty, along with strikes from Peter Ward and Gerry Ryan, made it 3-0 to the Seagulls.

WEDNESDAY 26th DECEMBER 1990

The match with Bristol Rovers was played in torrential rain at the Goldstone Ground. The visitors won 1-0. The programme identified a new member of the board; 46-year-old Bill Archer. "It's a great honour to be asked to join the board and I am really looking forward to becoming involved in professional sport again [he was instrumental in Liverpool's 1979 shirt sponsorship deal with Crown]. Brighton have terrific potential and I am here to develop a greater sponsorship input for the future."

FRIDAY 26th DECEMBER 1997

The Seagulls drew 4-4 – after being 3-0 down – against Colchester United at Gillingham. On-loan Paul Emblen scored a hat-trick. Albion have played 64 times on Boxing Day since entering the league. The record reads: won 35, drawn 14, lost 15, scored 114 and conceded 69.

Saturday 27th December 1930

Geordie Nicol netted four times in the 5-0 drubbing of Gillingham at the Goldstone. Dan Kirkwood was the other scorer during the win.

Saturday 27th December 1958

Promotion contenders Fulham visited Hove with former fans' favourite Jimmy Langley in their line-up. The largest crowd in Goldstone history – 36,747 – enjoyed a 3-0 win. Tommy Dixon (2) and Adrian Thorne were on target in Albion's inaugural second division campaign.

Saturday 27th December 1980

In an enthralling first division encounter, Albion beat Crystal Palace 3-2 at the Goldstone. Peter O'Sullivan and Michael Robinson (2) were the goalscorers in front of 27,367 fans.

Tuesday 27th December 1983

'The dirtiest player in Europe' made his debut against Fulham. Dutchman Hans Kraay arrived at the club with a somewhat tarnished reputation after pushing over a referee while playing for NAC Breda. Very popular with Albion fans, Kraay was sent off twice in 23 appearances. He is fondly remembered for jumping in front of opposition goalkeepers at corners.

Friday 28th December 1973

The birthdate of Jeff Minton in London. The midfielder arrived on a free transfer from Tottenham Hotspur in 1994 and shone during a torrid time on and off the pitch. He eventually followed Brian Horton to Port Vale in 1990 after 32 goals in 198 appearances, a very credible tally.

Saturday 28th December 1985

A fourth successive game on the road resulted in a surprise 3-2 victory at Leeds United. The second division contest was played in front of 13,011 fans at Elland Road as former Leeds player Terry Connor gave Chris Cattlin's team the lead. A rare Graham Pearce goal secured the win.

Monday 28th December 1998

A brace from Richie Barker secured the points in a 2-1 victory at Peterborough. Bizarrely, 365 days earlier, the teams, the score and the venue were exactly the same!

SATURDAY 29th DECEMBER 1979

The programme versus Manchester City described a recent visit to Hove by world darts champion Eric Bristow. 'Among the gathering were Peter Ward and a young Gary Stevens and, as Eric beat all 16 opponents, they joined the amazement at the skill of a man reputed to earn £1,000 a week from a sport renowned for the beer capacity of its participants. Peter and Gary restricted themselves to a small lager and a bitter lemon respectively.'

MONDAY 29th DECEMBER 1981

Striker Michael Robinson borrowed the Father Christmas costume he wore the previous day at a children's party for the players' festive knees-up. Gary Williams turned up dressed as Wurzel Gummidge.

SATURDAY 30th DECEMBER 1911

Jimmy Smith, who was born in the Potteries, scored all four goals as Albion beat Southern League newcomers Stoke 4-0 at the Goldstone.

SATURDAY 30th DECEMBER 1989

Former England winger Mark Barham donned the stripes for the first time in the 1-0 home defeat to Oxford United. The winger was signed from West Bromwich Albion by Barry Lloyd – who considered him his best signing during his time as boss of Albion. Barham provided excellent ammunition for Mike Small and John Byrne during the play-off season of 1990/91. He joined Shrewsbury Town in May 1992.

SATURDAY 31st DECEMBER 1927

Micky Kavanagh was born in Dublin on this date. The little forward went to Hull City for a trial as a 16-year-old. When no-one met him at the local train station, a friendly policeman let the Irishman spend his first night in England in a police box. He arrived in Hove in 1948 and, unfortunately, only managed seven strikes in 27 starts after severing his knee ligaments to prompt early retirement at the age of 22.

SATURDAY 31st DECEMBER 1955

Former sailor Malcolm Stephens scored twice as Albion beat Aldershot 3-0 in the third division (south). Des Tennant also found the target as Billy Lane's men stayed third.